Sound and Acupuncture

Also in the Star to Cell series by Fabien Maman

Book I :   *The Role of Music in the Twenty-First Century*

Book II: *Raising Human Frequencies:*
              The Way of Chi and the Subtle Bodies

Book IV: *Healing with Sound, Color and Movement:*
              Nine Evolutionary Healing Techniques

From Star to Cell:
A Sound Structure for the Twenty-First Century

Book III

The Body as a Harp
Sound and Acupuncture

Fabien Maman

Sound and Acupuncture

Fabien Maman

Published by:

Tama-Dõ Press
2060 Las Flores Canyon
Malibu, CA 90265
800.615.3675
info@tama-do.com
www.tamado.com

Copyright © 1997 by Fabien Maman
All rights reserved. No part of this book may be reproduced or transmitted electronically or mechanically, including photocopying, recording or by any information or retrieval system without written permission from the author, except for the inclusion of brief quotations in review.

Reprint: 2005

Cover Illustration by Hilary Pearson
Typography and Graphic Design by David Haefeli and Coloria S à r.l.
Illustrations by Jean-Luc Haldimann of Coloria S à r.l.
Copy Editing by Cynthia Reber Maman and Susan Klopman
Printed in Poland by Morpol

Library of Congress Catalog Card Number 97-90565

ISBN 0-9657714-2-3

Disclaimer

The healing techniques described in this book are not intended as a substitute for regular medical attention. In addition, Fabien Maman, Tama-Dõ Press and the Academy of Sound, Color and Movement cannot be held responsible for the results of the use of these methods when practiced without proper training as taught by the Academy of Sound, Color and Movement.

For Sensei Nakazono

With Gratitude

Without the help of Cynthia Reber Maman, this book would not have been written. The entire series of books, *From Star to Cell: A Sound Structure for the Twenty-First Century,* represents hundreds of teaching cassette tapes from many different countries which Cynthia transcribed and then worked with me to put into English and book form. It was truly a joint effort as well as a monumental task of commitment, dedication and love.

Acknowledgements

I would like to thank all of the students of the Academy of Sound, Color and Movement and especially Mary Pout and Hilary Pearson for computer charts and artwork, Patricia Janus for her "guided" support and color research, Dr. Patrick Camus for the generous sharing of his color research as well as his home when we needed a place to write, Jean Allen for her acupuncture input and Jeff Chitourus who said early on that "this stuff should be in a book" and has offered support and advice throughout the project. A special thanks to Christina Ross for her continuous enthusiasm and gracious willingness be of service no matter what the task and to Harry and Mary Reber who offered their hospitality, their "sound/storage studio" and suppport throughout the process.

Thanks also to David, Frédéric and Jean-Luc of Coloria of Switzerland who supplied their gifts for computer graphics and to Susan Klopman for her editing skills. I am also grateful to Dr. Rene Gandolfi for his early and immediate recognition of the value of this work and for his continual friendship and support. Finally, my deep appreciation to the source of the inspiration I have received for my work and my life.

Contents

		page
Preface		XIV
Introduction	*The Body as a Harp*	XVI

Chapter One **1**
The Way of Nature: Chinese Five Element Theory

- *Why Chinese Medicine?* — 2
- *The Pulse of Life* — 7
- *Chinese Energetic Clock* — 8
- *Characteristics of the Five Elements* — 9
- *Emotions and the Five Elements* — 20
- *Voice Quality and the Five Elements* — 22

Chapter Two **29**
The Spiritual Essence of the Five Elements: The Five Shen

- *Explanation of the Shen Ideogram* — 32
- *The Will and the Five Shen* — 42
- *Musical Link, Earth to Sky:* — 42
  Acoustic Instruments, the Five Elements and the Five Shen

Chapter Three **45**
Organic Psychology: The Psychology of the Temperaments

- *The Six Temperaments* — 46
- *General Treatment Information for the Six Temperaments* — 64

Chapter Four — 67
Sound and Acupuncture

- *Tuning Forks on Meridians* — 67
- *Tuning Forks and Shu Points* — 72
- *The Tuning Fork Technique* — 76
- *Sound and the Spiral of the Ear* — 79
- *Using Tuning Forks on Ear Points* — 80
- *The Musical Spine* — 84

Chapter Five — 89
Kototama Sound and Acupuncture

- *Kototama, Science of Pure Sound* — 89
- *Sound Structures: Space and Time* — 92
- *Kototama Sounds and Acupuncture* — 93
- *The Song of the Triple Warmer* — 96

Chapter Six — 99
The Chart of the Eight Elements

- *The Meaning of the Three Ethers* — 100
- *Analogy of the Musical Structures Corresponding to the Elements* — 103

Chapter Seven — 107
Prenatal Alchemical Etheric Cycle

- *Synchronization* — 111
- *Integration* — 116
- *Transformation* — 117
- *The Etheric Chart* — 118

Appendix — 127

Preface

The series of books, *From Star to Cell: A Sound Structure for the Twenty-First Century* evolved out of the merging of my musical background with the study and practice of acupuncture, Kototama (Science of Pure Sound), martial arts and research in bioenergetics.

As I learned the laws of the vibrational world in the body through work with energy in acupuncture and Aikido I became more tuned to the invisible worlds of the subtle bodies and sound. I began to sense the formation of a subtle design based on music, acupuncture and my work in laboratory with cells and sound (shown in Book I, *The Role of Music in the Twenty-First Century*) which links human beings through resonance to nature and the cosmos.

This living structure is based in the physical body on the laws of acupuncture and continues through the five elements of nature to the subtle bodies and even to the vibrational essence of cosmic energy. Through the frequencies of the subtle bodies, we have a link with high energetic information. The acupuncture base in the physical body insures that even the highest vibrational messages can actually be integrated physically through the correct channels, or acupuncture meridians.

Without a base in human anatomy, vibrational tools for healing such sound, color and movement have no anchor in physical reality. I have found that the energetic anatomical structure of the human being in resonance with nature offered by Chinese Oriental Medicine provides an excellent foundation for the integration of healing work with sound.

This book, the third in the series, explores the acupuncture and sound foundation of my work. Chapters One and Two develop aspects of the Law of the Five Elements of Chinese Oriental Medicine which form the principles behind acupuncture and into which I have integrated possibilities with sound healing. Chapter Three describes the psychology of the temperaments. Chapter Four explores techniques for using sound in acupuncture. Chapters Five explores the link between the sounds of Kototama, the Science of Pure Sound, and acupuncture, Chapters Six and Seven continue the relationship between sound and acupuncture by offering a new synthesis which M.D. and Acupuncturist Dominique Eraud of Paris describes as a sort of "celestial acupuncture." In these final chapters I propose a tool for divination which places the human being at birth in resonance with the greater energy patterns of sky and earth which will influence lifelong physical, psychological and spiritual temperament.

I offer this book to acupuncturists and non-acupuncturists alike as a resource for the new and promising field of sound healing.

Fabien Maman
Autumn, 1997
Vevey, Switzerland

Introduction

The Body as a Harp

I was first introduced to acupuncture while I was a musician in the 1970s. During a musical performance tour of Japan our group of five musicians arrived at the New Otani Hotel in Tokyo completely exhausted. We had been traveling for over twenty-four hours from Paris. Our first concert was to begin in a few hours. I asked at the hotel desk for a masseuse to rejuvenate us before the concert. There were no masseuses available on such short notice. Instead, the hotel clerk sent us a very old acupuncturist.

He told us all to lie down on the floor of the hotel room and began to insert little needles up and down our bodies. In twenty minutes I could feel my energy returning. I asked the acupuncturist what he was doing, why he put needles in this place and not in another and how they could work so fast. He explained in rudimentary English that the body was filled with lines of energy, like rivers, and he was choosing certain important channels in which to place the needles.

As he spoke I had a vision of the body as a musical harp. The strings of the harp were the lines of energy in the body. And just as the harpist plays on the strings of the harp, so the acupuncturist was playing on the energy meridians of the body. I remember looking at the acupuncturist and thinking, "he is the real musician in this room."

When I returned to France from this tour, I entered a school of acupuncture. I had intended to put my performance career on the back burner for six months while I learned enough about healing to keep our quintet of musicians healthy while we traveled. I never could have guessed that twenty years later this performance career would still be on hold!

Sound and Acupuncture

Though I had reduced my performance traveling in order to remain in Paris and study acupuncture and Aikido, music still remained central to me and little by little I gained another understanding of what sound and music can be for human beings.

I was learning the laws of the vibrational world in the body through work with energy in acupuncture and Aikido. The more I worked with energy, the more tuned I became to the invisible worlds of the subtle bodies and sound. Furthermore, I found that the laws of acupuncture provide a practical anatomical basis in the physical body for integrating healing work with sound. This places the possibilities for the resonance of sound and the human being within the natural and precise spiral of energy linking the human being, nature and the cosmos.

Chapter One

The Way of Nature: Chinese Five Element Theory

...I wish to hear the story of the bones and the marrow, about the viscera and about the liver and the lungs...I urge you to bring into harmony for me Nature, Heaven, and Tao, the right way.

There must be an end and a beginning. Heaven must be in accord with the lights of the sky, the celestial bodies, and their course and periods. The earth below must reflect the four seasons, the five elements, that which is precious and that which is lowly and without value.

Is it not that in Winter man responds to Yin, the principle of darkness and cold? And is it not that in Summer he responds to Yang the principle of light and warmth? Let me be informed about their workings.

...so asked the Yellow Emperor of the T'ien Shih (Master of Heaven) the divinely inspired teacher

the Nei Ching Su Wên
The Yellow Emperor's Classic of Internal Medicine [1]

Why Chinese Medicine?

*Since the entire universe followed one
immutable course which became manifest
through the change of night to day,
through the recurrence of the seasons,
through growth and decay, man in his
utter dependence upon the universe could
not do better than to follow a way which
was conceived after that of nature.*[2]

It is this "way of nature" which became the living structure behind the human being's relationship to earth and heaven that is called acupuncture. Acupuncture has lasted for thousands of years and has been used by more human beings in the world than any other system of medicine. It is still working today.

There is pattern to the way that energy runs through nature, creating day and night, summer, fall, winter and spring, birth, decay, death and rebirth. The inner structure of energy which supports all forms of life must also support human life.

This principle is the beauty and simplicity of the Chinese system. Just as all human beings have a heart on the left side of the body and a liver on the right side of the body, so too all human beings have a universal structure of energy channels which bring vital essence, or chi, to the internal organs. These channels of energy are called meridians. The Chinese gave us this system of Energetic Anatomy. It is a system as precise and accurate as the textbook anatomy of Western medicine.

It is through this inner structure that we resonate with both the changing patterns of the sky and the cyclical seasons of earth. Our energies move inside the greater pattern; we are one with the whole.

The highest way of healing is through the use of pure chi. Because it is based upon the movement of chi through the meridians, acupuncture is irreplaceable in its central position of healing. Acupuncture links Tai Chi, Chi Gong, Tao Yin Fa and the Martial Arts to the possibility of self healing and human evolution.[3]

Energy is always moving. Consciousness evolves. Rigid structures are bound to crack with time. The beauty of the Chinese structure is that it is fluid enough to allow for continuity and expansion over time. The inner anatomy of the human being, based on energy, is a foundation which allows evolution into the finer energies of the subtle bodies.

The ideal of harmony permeates Chinese philosophy and medical orientation. We in the West, in contrast, strive for the Greek ideal of perfection rather than harmony. Like the Greek statues of old, this static ideal remains unmovable, uncompromising and unattainable. Obsession for perfection, especially physical perfection, sets ourselves up for failure no matter how hard we to try to achieve the unachievable. If we were to pursue the ideal of harmony, rather than perfection, we could find ourselves "perfect" at any stage of our lives.

THE FIVE ELEMENTS OF CHINESE MEDICINE

Yin and Yang, in addition to exerting their dual power, are subdivided into wood, fire, earth, metal, water. Man, who is said to be the product of heaven and earth by the interaction of Yin and Yang, also contains, therefore, the five elements.

The five elements were also distributed over the seasons: Each element was attached to a particular season; wood belonging to spring, fire to summer, metal to fall and water to winter.

Each season was thought to originate from one point of the compass; hence the element of each season was also the element of the direction from which the season originated.[4]

The five elements represent not only the essence of each season but also the stages of the manifestation of life on earth:

> In the birth phase of the earth arose wood - all growing matter.
>
> In the surging upward phase burned fire, - air and gases.
>
> In the mature adult phase appeared earth, - dirt and soil.
>
> In the decay phase came metal - all inorganic matter.
>
> In the death/rebirth phase sprung water, - all moisture.

The stages of manifestation of life on earth represent the creative (Sheng) cycle of the five elements which is shown by the clockwise flow of energy in the diagram below. In this circulation of energy, fire empowers earth, earth empowers metal, metal empowers water, water empowers wood and wood empowers fire. This cycle can be seen in nature: fire creates ash for earth, earth gives ground for the metals, metal gives vitality to water, water nourishes wood and wood is fuel for fire.

The cycle of energy represented by the arrows in the star formation in the diagram below is the control (Ke) cycle built into the universe. This cycle inhibits energy. Fire melts metal, metal cuts wood, wood "strangles" earth, earth absorbs and contains water, and water extinguishes fire.

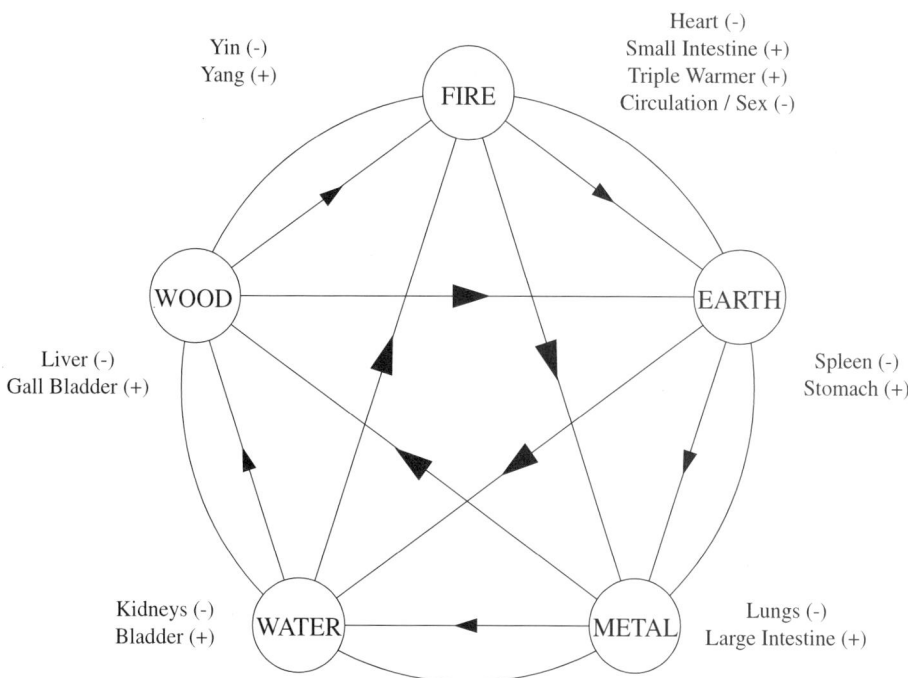

> *While the element that belonged to one season was at its height, the element connected with the previous season was waning, the element connected with the following season was waxing, and the fourth element was in temporary eclipse.*
>
> Nei Ching Su Wên [5]

We are linked to the five elements through our internal organs. Each season has its element which is the essential energy of that season. Each of our internal organs also resonates with the particular vibration of one of the elements and its season. Thus, our inner structure follows the laws which govern the five elements and the seasons.

The liver and gall bladder, for example, reach the height of their energies in the spring time. At the same time, the energy of the kidneys and bladder are waning from their fullness in the winter. The heart and small intestine energies are waxing, preparing for their moment of fullest vitality in the summer.

The Pulse of Life

By observing the laws of the five elements, we can re-establish contact with nature and the cosmos. This contact is not simply mental; it is a living communication. We can feel nature, the cycles and seasons, vibrating within our pulses. When taking the Chinese pulses on the inside of the wrist, acupuncturists also can feel whether internal energies are in balance with the season.

When the tender shoots burst their way through the ground in the excitement of spring, our own energies pulse through the inner channels, running tight and wiry, like the stem of a spring flower, vibrating like violin strings with the birth of springtime.

In the fullness of summer, when the fruit hangs heavy on the trees, the chi pulses, full and generous, through the channels to the internal organs of our bodies.

When autumn arrives, the trees, freed of their summer burden of fruit and leaves, are lighter and so is the pulse of the energy flowing through the inner pathways of the body.

In the cold and dark of the winter, our pulses rest deep, internal, difficult to find, like the seed waiting in the deep cold wet underground of winter.

When we are healthy our energy pulses in tune with the season. When we are not healthy, it is because we have fallen out of harmony with the season. With their understanding of the Laws of the Five Elements, the Sheng Cycle and Ke Cycle, acupuncturists can help to bring internal energies back into harmony with the season.

Sound and Acupuncture

The Chinese Energetic Clock

The elements of nature ebb and flow also according to a twenty-four hour cycle within the seasonal rhythmic changes. Within this twenty-four hour cycle the energy of the body moves through the internal organs in the same natural flow as the gradual turning of day into night.

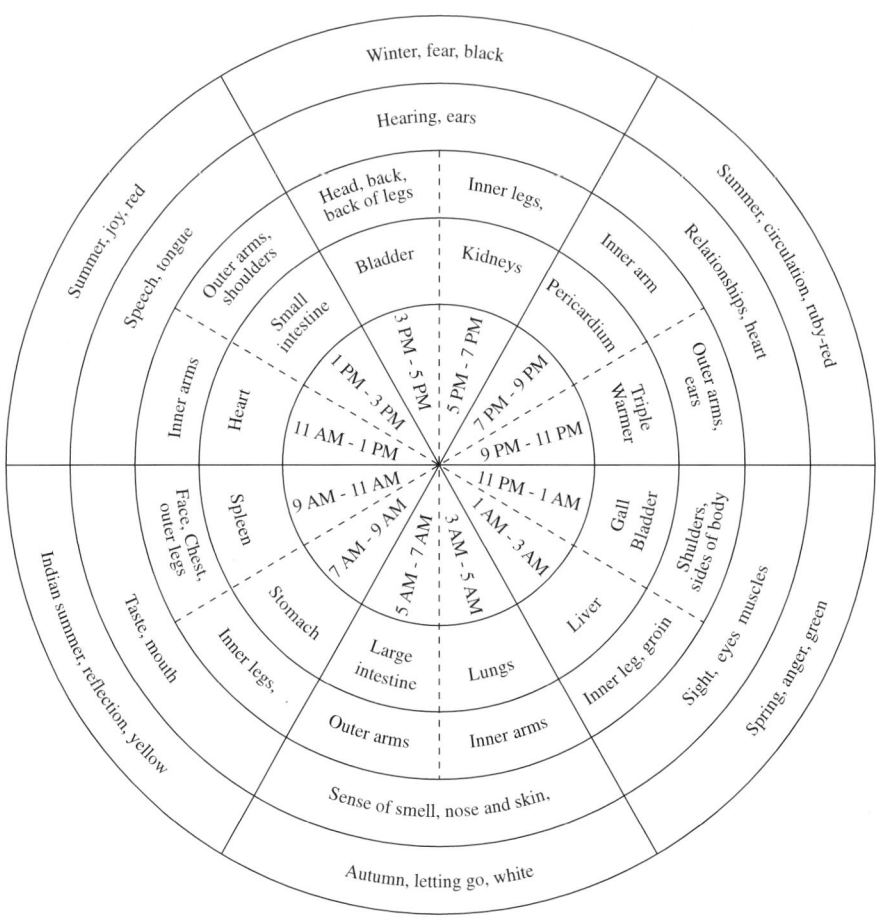

Many people are unconsciously aware that the energy runs through the body in this cycle without ever reading a Chinese clock. We break-fast in the morning between seven and nine o'clock when the energy comes into the stomach. The Triple Warmer sexual energy is highest in the evening between 9:00 p.m. and 11:00 p.m.

Characteristics of the Five Elements According to the Nei Ching Su Wên

WOOD

Liver   1:00 a.m. - 3:00 a.m.   YIN
Gall Bladder   11:00 p.m. - 1:00 a.m.   YANG

SEASON	Spring
COLOR	Green
DIRECTION	East
ODOR	Rancid
TASTE	Sour
SOUND	Shouting
EMOTION	Anger
POWER	Birth
CLIMATE	Wind
FORTIFIES	Ligaments
PULSE	2nd of left hand - tight wiry
NOTE	A
MODE	Aeolian
SOUND	a - wa

Wood, linked with the eyes:

Characteristics: Rooted, growing, flexible, durable, contains the flow of life, carries the seeds of new life, strong, yielding to the wind, sensitive, vital, full of fervor and will power. Can be disturbed in the spring by the wind.

Pulse: The quality of the pulse must be like a plant in the spring as it grows out of the seed - tight. The stem is tight, long, but empty. Tight but subtle is the principle quality of the pulse of the spring. If the pulse is not in this condition there is cause for concern. It should be taut like the string of a violin.

Negative Aspects: Anger, not seeing clearly, feeling off balance or falling over, feeling disconnected with earth, dizzy, uprooted, confused, lacking the ability to create roots for oneself, vertigo.

Common Disorders: Paralysis, arthritis, stultifying thoughts and emotions, feelings of being smothered or trapped, abdominal pains, cramps, weak limbs and trunk, lack of the ability to plan. The coleduc (duct between gall bladder and intestine) gets stuck with "mud" (especially with fasting, stress or anger).

The **Liver** is a "strategic planner." The function of the liver is to metabolize fats and break down toxins in the body. Malfunction of the liver causes digestive problems, nausea, jaundice, hepatitis, nearsightedness. Mentally, a liver malfunction causes aimlessness, bad planning, no sense of direction or purpose, inability to make plans.

An excess of energy in the liver leads to overplanning, obsession, rigidity, insensitivity to change, the making of large ambitious plans which are unable to be fulfilled or which never get off the ground.

Spiritually, a malfunctioning liver creates hopelessness, the inability to move ahead, lack of drive and self assertion, suicidal tendencies.

The **Gall Bladder** is the "decision maker." Its function is to emulsify fats through the use of bile.

When the gall bladder is not functioning properly there may be lack of co-ordination, clumsiness, accident proneness, frustration, anger, aggression, eye problems, migraines, indecisiveness, stuckness, despair.

The small intestine depends upon the gall bladder for digestion, the Triple Heater depends upon the gall bladder's healthy regulation of temperature, while the stomach, the bladder and the colon each needs a "decision" as to when they are empty or full.

FIRE

Heart	11:00 a.m. to 1:00 p.m.	YIN
Small Intestines	1:00 p.m. to 3:00 p.m.	YANG
Pericardium		
(Circulation Sex)	7:00 p.m. to 9:00 p.m.	YIN
Triple Warmer	9:00 p.m. to 11:00 p.m.	YANG

SEASON	Summer	
COLOR	Red	
DIRECTION	South	
ODOR	Burnt, scorched	
TASTE	Bitter, hot	
SOUND	Laughing, singing, low voice, drawn out, belching	
EMOTION	Joy	
POWER	Maturity	
CLIMATE	Heat	
FORTIFIES	Arteries	
PULSE	1st of left hand, 3rd on right - big, "flooded", not tight, scattered	
NOTE	C	E
MODE	Ionian	Byzantine
SOUND	e - we	hi - hwi

Fire, linked with the tongue:

Characteristics: Jolly, full of excitement, enthusiastic, active, alive, sparkling, ablaze, warm, generous, loving, vital, happy, needs a constant controlled source of fuel, larger-than life, big-hearted, inner joy, communication, relationship, growth.

Pulse: Must be like a flower in summer. Full, heavy, generous. If it is too tight, or too soft, there is a fire imbalance.

Negative Aspects: Cold physically, emotionally and sexually when the fire has "gone out." Hot, "burning," painful joints. Parched and arid mind, body and spirit. Lack of receptivity, poor circulation, varicose veins, hemorrhoids, hot flashes, heartburn and digestive problems, bent and contracted muscles, numbness, temperature problems, stuttering, deafness, panic, paranoia. Low or excess vitality. Mentally, when the fire is not balanced in the body, there may be helplessness, self-pity, neglect of responsibilities, insecurity, loneliness, serious mindedness, coldness, withdrawal, lack of clarity, inability to concentrate, joylessness or inappropriate joy, apathy, depression, despair.

The **Heart** is called in the *Nei Ching* the "monarch who excels through insight and understanding." When functioning well, the heart creates vitality, energy and joy for the body. When malfunctioning, there is panic, chaos, disorder, jumbled speech, stuttering, incoherence and rambling.

The **Small Intestine** creates changes in physical substance. In its function as a sorter, it separates the pure from the impure. When functioning well, the small intestine sorts through all incoming food and selectively absorbs that which is of value. It sends what is valuable through the blood and that which is not valuable through the colon. On other levels we could say that the small intestine is responsiblity for the ability to sort through incoming information and ideas, absorbing what is useful and rejecting what is not.

When the small intestine is not functioning well, a person may experience obesity or extreme thinness, toxic build up, swellings, painful joints, blood disorders, hearing problems and deafness. Mentally, one becomes lazy, vague, can't get a grip on things, the mind wanders. Spiritually, a person may be confused and may follow many different gurus.

The **Pericardium (Circulation Sex)** is the protector of the heart and the guide of joy and pleasure. The function of the pericardium is to control the blood flow in the arteries and veins, to control the internal and external sexual secretions and to act as a barrier to protect the heart from abuse and shock. It is responsible for oxygenating the blood.

When the pericardium is not functioning well there are circulation problems, blood pressure problems, angina, arrhythmia, varicose veins, hemorrhoids, and frozen joints. Mentally there is shyness or aloofness.

The **Triple Warmer,** or Triple Heater, maintains temperature and warmth at optimum conditions for the whole system. The function of the Triple Warmer is to work with the immune system and distribute the white corpuscles in the blood. When the Triple Warmer is not functioning well there can be dry skin, redness, blotches, spots, cold hands and feet, circulation problems, varicose veins, hormonal imbalances, rheumatoid arthritis, swelling joints, hypothermia, hyperthermia and sweating.

Mentally there can be a lack of communication in social situations, an inability to cope with social change, lack of warmth, discontentedness, edginess, irritation, emotional instability, irrational thoughts or unpredictability. Also, when the Triple Warmer is malfunctioning, there is depression, withdrawal, apathy and resignation on a spiritual level.

Sound and Acupuncture

EARTH

Spleen   9:00 a.m. to 11:00 a.m. YIN
Stomach   7:00 a.m. to 9:00 a.m.   YANG

SEASON	Indian summer
COLOR	Yellow
DIRECTION	Center
ODOR	Fragrant
TASTE	Sweet
SOUND	Singing
EMOTION	Sympathy
POWER	Decrease
CLIMATE	Humidity
FORTIFIES	Muscles
PULSE	2nd on right
	Moderate, big
NOTE	F
MODE	Lydian
SOUND	i - wi

Earth, linked with the mouth and lips:

Characteristics: Nourishing, supportive, fertile, full, abundant, ripe, stable, basic, rounded, cyclic, centered, grounded, balanced, comfortable, reflective, sympathetic, firm, strong, free from obsession, at ease, dependable, self-sufficient, interacting and connected with the source.

Pulse: Firm and strong. When imbalanced, it has the feel of perishing fruit.

Negative Aspects: When the earth is out of balance there can be too much reflection, overthinking. There is no self discipline and often clinging (to mother principle), or dependency.

Common Disorders: Ulcers, anorexia, indigestion, obesity, vomiting, hyperacidity, sweet tooth, problems with the menstrual cycle, nervousness, flightiness, instability, loss of balance.

The function of the Spleen is to distribute, transport and transform energy. The spleen absorbs nutrition which has been taken in by the stomach and broken down by the liver and gall bladder. It then distributes the energy of food in all directions of the body. The spleen has an important role in the blood circulation and supply of food to the muscles. It helps the organs remain in position and transforms mental processes.

When the spleen is malfunctioning there could be diabetes, hypoglycemia or hyperglycemia, all of which have to do with sugar in the body. There could also be sluggish circulation, clogging of the blood, varicose veins, hernias, loss of libido. Mentally, thoughts can go "round and round;" there can be a lack of mental and emotional stimulation with unpredictable and irregular energy.

The **Stomach** acts as a place of accumulation for water and food and as a source of supply for the bowels. Food is digested here. The function of the stomach is to receive and process nourishment, to integrate it and pass on the food energy to be distributed by the spleen. The stomach is linked with assimilation, memory and concentration.

When the stomach is not functioning properly, the results are poor appetite, dyspepsia, acidity, nausea, vomiting, ulcers, abdominal pain, Bell's palsy, energy depletion, lethargy, digestive problems, weakness and debilitation. Mentally there can be an the inability to concentrate or to remember. The mind becomes sluggish, heavy and unable to shift repetitive thoughts, worries and ideas which can become distorted and obsessive.

METAL

Lungs: 3:00 a.m. to 5:00 a.m.   YIN
Large Intestines: 5:00 a.m. to 7:00 a.m. YANG

SEASON	Autumn
COLOR	White
DIRECTION	West
ODOR	Rotten
TASTE	Pungent, spicy
SOUND	Weeping
EMOTION	Grief
POWER	Balance
CLIMATE	Dryness
FORTIFIES	Skin and hair
PULSE	Floating, Rough, short
NOTE	G
MODE	Mixolydian
SOUND	u - wu

Metal, linked with the nose and the skin:

Characteristics: Minerals provide substance and richness, intensity of earth, fuel for heat, material structure for strength, gems for beauty. Metal provides then substance, strength and structure, reinforcement, bolstering, uprightness, provides system of communication and materials for means of construction.

Negative Aspects include a lack of structure and strength, lack of emotional strength, breakdown in communications which cause dissension and disintegration, withering.

Pulse: Light but slightly rough feeling.

Common Disorders: Rheumatic pains, degeneration or rigidity of the vertebral column, specific kinds of headaches, trembling, spasms of the throat, esophagus and limbs, paralysis, debilitating diseases, lack of emotional strength, incoherent speech.

The **Lungs** are the organs of respiration which affect all of the rhythms in the body including blood flow. They take in life force, chi from nature and the cosmos.

When the lungs are not healthy the symptoms include asthma, bronchitis, coughing, dry throat, raspiness, shortness of breath, congestion, tuberculosis, pleurisy, sinus problems, emphysema, eczema, psoriasis, rashes, speech problems.

The **Large Intestines** are the organs of elimination, cleanliness and purity, of evacuation of physical waste and the ability to surrender. When the large intestines are not healthy there can be diarrhea, bloatedness, swelling, constipation, emotional blockages, acne, boils, headache, stuffy nose, weight loss, dehydration, accumulation of unnecessary physical possessions. Mentally there can be a refusal to let go of grievances. Spiritual issues appear cloudy.

WATER

Kidneys: 5:00 p.m. to 7:00 p.m. YIN
Bladder: 3:00 p.m. to 5:00 p.m. YANG

SEASON	Winter
COLOR	Black
DIRECTION	North
ODOR	Putrid
TASTE	Salty
SOUND	Groaning
EMOTION	Fear
POWER	Emphasis
CLIMATE	Cold
FORTIFIES	Bones
PULSE	Slippery, soggy
NOTE	D
MODE	Dorian
SOUND	o - wo

Water, linked with the ears and bones:

Characteristics: Cold, warm, clear, force and power, rhythm and cycle, serene, submissive, nourishing, sustaining, refreshing, revitalizing, a life principle, a basis for travel, softness, gentleness, intuition, inner vision.

Negative Aspects: Violent, inundating, overwhelming, cold, dark, fearful, murky

Pulse: In winter the seed prepares for growth. It rests deep underground and in water. Therefore, the pulse must be strong, deep and resistant.

Common Disorders: Brittleness of joints, dryness and thirst, frequency or infrequency of urination, excess or deficiency of perspiration, saliva, tears, sexual secretions and lactation. Fear of heights, water, people, sexuality, enclosed spaces, new things, darkness and death. Anxiety.

The **Kidney** is the storehouse of the vital essence and the largest accumulator of energy in the body. When the kidneys are drained they refill during sleep. If one third of the kidney energy reserve is empty this results in depression. If two thirds of the kidney reserve is empty there is madness. If all of the kidney reserve is empty, death is near.

The function of the kidneys is to regulate the amount of water in the body, to bathe the entire cellular system, aid the endocrine system and excrete urine. When there is a kidney malfunction the symptoms include swelling, bloating, sharp pains, difficulty urinating, inability to digest food, high blood pressure, hypertension, and chills. There would be a lack of flow in the thought processes and in the emotions. Energy leaks away. There could also be tremendous anxiety, fear of everything, stress and depression.

The **Bladder** eliminates fluid waste, stores the overflow and the fluid secretions which serve to regulate vaporization. The function of the bladder is to store the fluids to excrete and help the kidneys store the vital essence. When the bladder is malfunctioning there is the inability to urinate, depression, impotence, frigidity, inability to cope with life, and lack of adaptability.

Emotions and the Five Elements

There are many qualities that belong to each of the five elements. In addition to season, internal organ, color, sound and direction, a specific emotional energy can be added to the Five Element Sheng and Ke Cycles.

When emotion can be understood not only psychologically, but as energy representing the qualities of the elements, we can address the fluid essence of emotion and are able to move with it by applying the Laws of the Five Elements:

	IN EXCESS	IN BALANCE
The quality of wood =	anger	creativity
The quality of fire =	overexcitement	joy
The quality of earth =	worry	stability
The quality of metal =	sadness	compassion
The quality of water =	fear	wisdom

By applying these qualities onto the Five Element Sheng and Ke Cycles, the circle and the star, emotional energy or blocks could be affected by working, not directly with emotion, but with the elements and even with the corresponding organs.

For example, imagine a person whose anger is consistently inappropriate or out of control. To confront this anger directly or to look into the past to find the origin of the anger does little to actually move this energy.

Just as metal cuts wood in the Ke cycle of the five elements, work with the metal element or with the lungs and large intestine energies would release the power of sadness which heals and balances the anger of the wood.

Five Elements and Emotional Chi

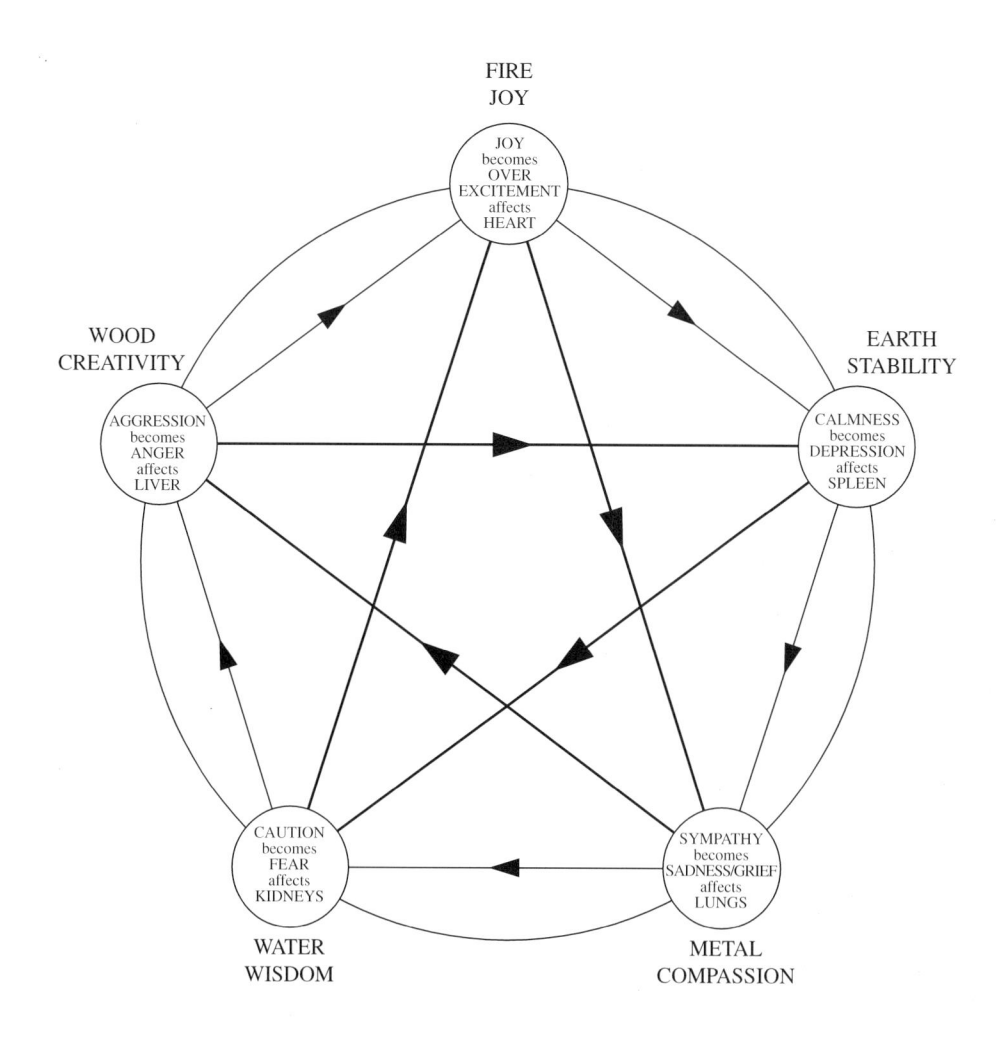

FIRE
JOY

JOY becomes OVER EXCITEMENT affects HEART

WOOD
CREATIVITY

AGGRESSION becomes ANGER affects LIVER

EARTH
STABILITY

CALMNESS becomes DEPRESSION affects SPLEEN

CAUTION becomes FEAR affects KIDNEYS

SYMPATHY becomes SADNESS/GRIEF affects LUNGS

WATER
WISDOM

METAL
COMPASSION

The chi of joy is stronger than the chi of sadness. Sadness wins over anger. Anger kills reason. Reason cancels fear and fear destroys joy.

Voice Quality and the Five Elements

The sound of the voice reflects many of the essential aspects and qualities of the inner vibration which represents each person's individual makeup. The voice expresses most immediately a person's true emotional and energetic state whether or not the words represent this state.

The voice expresses "perfectly" inner fear, anger, sadness or joy and reveals even more subtle nuances which are related not only to emotion, but to level of consciousness. When we hear a voice, we hear not only feelings and opinions, but also the authentic level of consciousness of the speaker which is present regardless of the words which are spoken.

A voice can be high pitched or low pitched. It can speak slowly or fast. It can inspire and give energy, or be boring and drain energy. It can incite anger and nervousness or be a soothing calming influence.

The quality of voice, like emotion, can also be linked with one of the five elements and is influenced by the Laws of the Five Elements including the Sheng Cycle of empowerment and the Ke Cycle of inhibition.

The qualities inherent in each element can be reflected in the voice as follows:

- Wood Voice: Soft, muted, gentle.
- Fire Voice: Rising and falling, breathless (inhaling a lot, trying to catch the breath).
- Earth Voice: Resonating bass, enveloping, firm, can slow one down.
- Metal Voice: Sharp, metallic with a high pitched resonance.
- Water Voice: Continuously talking (not necessarily fast), linking subjects endlessly, allowing no breaks, lamenting sound, demanding, draining. Often water voices follow their own monologue and drain energy from others because they leave no space for interaction.

Wood

A wood voice can be muted or vibrant, but it is always soft. Wood people are extremely sensitive to all other elements. Metal cuts wood, fire burns wood, water can overwhelm wood. Earth is the only element where wood can feel safe and quiet. The wood is vibrant, but it needs quiet.

Fire

The fire voice speaks through inhaling. This is the opposite of a water voice which speaks on the exhale. The fire voice will be awakening because energy is lifted through the inhalation. The fire voice will amplify the difference between the listener's emotional state and the natural exuberance carried by the fire element. The role of the fire voice is to transmit joy. In unbalanced states, the fire voice can create an excess of happiness, almost hysteria, which can be overwhelming to the heart.

Earth

The earth element is heavy, quiet, slow moving and implies a reflective nature. The earth voice will be low pitched, calming, secure. The rhythm of speaking will carry these qualities. This element attracts respect and inspires in the listener deep self-reflection. Earth is the only element which can stop the overwhelming aspect of water. In excess, an earth voice can become so slow that it makes others depressed. The earth person won't know he or she is depressing. Usually the vibrational expression of the voice is unrecognizable to the person who is speaking; others, however, can recognize easily the qualities hidden to the person whose voice it is.

Metal

A typical metal person will speak with a high, metallic voice, and a cutting vibration which wants everything clear immediately, even when this hurts people. These people will walk sharply, not smoothly. They can become mesmerized by the strong resonance of their own voice. (I am here. Listen to me). They can talk just for the love of the resonance of their own voice in their head. A metal voice can be a overwhelming for other people in public places such as plane, trains, restaurants, elevators!

People with metal voices make good teachers because they can keep a class awake. Their voices command attention and would help them to be effective leaders.

The role of metal people is to bring clarity of vision. If they misuse their gift, the high pitched voice can create hyper brain stimulation. They can become obsessed and overly meticulous through the resonance of their voice because they are naturally attached to detail.

Water

The water voice is soft, slow and continuously linking words, ideas and events. One word leads to the next. It is difficult to interrupt a water voice. This can be draining for the listener when the voice is in a crying or a fearful mood. The water voice speaks by exhaling. In excess, this exhalation becomes the sighing of sadness. The role of a water based person is to bring wisdom through the link with memory.

Voices in Relationship

The voice reflects the general temperament of a person. Using the Five Element Star which depicts the Ke Cycle of inhibition, we can imagine the challenges in relationships between people of different temperaments. For example, a person with a strong metal voice, sharp and cutting, will hurt the sensibility of a wood based person because metal chops wood. The vibratory tendency of metal to cut wood will be accentuated in relationship conflicts.

In a couple, when the initial attraction has begun to wear off and each one begins to pay attention to the personal details they overlooked before, the sound and quality of the voice will have a strong, albeit sometimes unconscious affect. For example, an earth voice, low and quiet, will contain a water voice. When conflict becomes extreme between an earth based person and a water based person, the water person will feel stifled and trapped.

A fire voice rises and falls quickly, like dancing flames. It inhales strongly and speaks a lot. A metal based person will feel as if his energy is being swallowed. Because fire melts metal, a metal based person will have difficulty with a fire voice. The metal person needs clarity and time for the resonance of the voice to be expressed. During relationship conflict, the metal person will not find the space he or she needs with a fire based person.

Harmony

In different states of relationship at work or at home, when love, compassion and understanding remain the guiding impulses of the relationship, the beneficial aspect of each of the five voice types will be expressed. This harmony follows the Sheng Cycle in the Law of the Five Elements.

> A metal voice gives clarity and resonance.
>
> A water voice offers kindness and understanding.
>
> A wood voice carries a soft and vibrant vibration.
>
> A fire voice brings enthusiasm and loving vibration.
>
> An earth voice offers stillness and security.

These voice qualities are depicted by element, but this explanation does not mean that a person cannot possess varying degrees of each quality. The quality missing in the elements will be provided by another aspect of the personality.

For example, a person who is a strong metal type will be very mental and sharp. He or she can also contain enthusiasm and love, a vibration that comes more naturally with the fire element. We may find this quality in another aspect of the personality, it just will not be expressed so clearly by the voice.

Just as the voice of each person reflects one or two of the five elements more strongly, so the overall temperament of each person is constituted with different balances of each element as Chapter Three explains. A person may reflect, perhaps, mostly wood and fire in his make-up and this would make him very different from one who resonated more with water.

We are born with our temperament. It is our physiological make-up that determines whether we resonate with the universe of wood in spring or water in winter. Our inner anatomy, our internal organs determine the elements which resonate through our voice and our path through life. We cannot change our make-up. It is our gift.

Though each person reflects the five elements differently, we each contain all five elements. When every person goes into the forest or sees the color green, or takes a walk on the first day of spring, the liver and gall bladder receives energy. When every person sits in the sun, the heart and small intestine are revitalized. When every person breathes the prana in the morning, lungs and large intestine respond. It helps during times of conflict to understand the mechanism of relationship at the vibrational level. This will bring the balance which allows love the space to bring the real answer: Love can harmonize all differences.

Chapter Two

The Spiritual Essence of the Five Elements: The Five Shen

The five elements in Chinese Medicine, which link human beings organically to the five elements of nature have subtle counterparts in the Five Shen, which are the "spiritual essences" of the five elements. The Chinese call the Five Shen the "doorway to the heavens." The resonance between the five elements of nature and the five "spiritual essences" allows for the newer research on subtle bodies and sound and color healing to be introduced into Chinese Medicine, taking it to higher vibrational levels without disturbing the basic structure.

The Shen link cosmic energy, the five elements and the organs of the body. It is through the Shen that the cosmic energy, or divine energy, of the elements makes its way to the internal organs. The energy from the cosmos is too strong to be received directly by the body. We need a medium to transform the qualities of cosmic energies that are transmitted to an internal organ of the body.

For example, we cannot just open our mouths and eat the sun! The cosmic energy of the sun must be transmuted by the fire element of the heart before it reaches the body. The cosmic energy of the moon must be transformed by the water element, through liquid, to the kidneys. So it is with any type of cosmic energy - the Shen must transmute this energy through the five elements in order for it to be useful on the physical level. The Shen serve the internal organs as well as the five elements in order to transmit, transform or translate messages between the two.

In Chinese Medicine cosmic energy, or "sky energy" corresponds to the yang aspect of the human being. It is through the breath, the "spiritual wind," of the human being that we are in resonance with sky energy. Earth represents yin energy. The blood is the yin aspect of the human being, our connection with earth. Messages are constantly traveling between the blood and the breath, from yin to yang, and from inside the body to the five elements of nature through the Shen to cosmic energy and back again to the body.

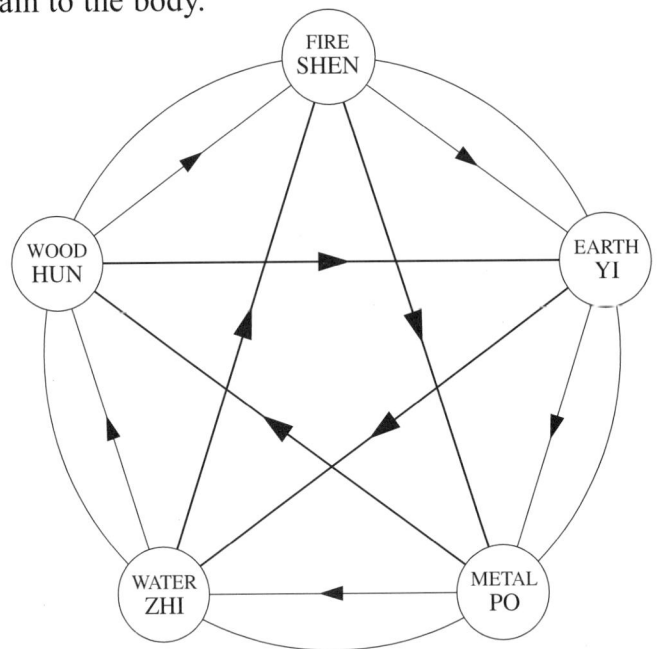

Shen	Element	Governs	To Excess	Lack of
Shen	Fire	Emotions	Timid, shy complaining	Madness
Yi	Earth	Reflection/thinking	Obsession with past, stiff, rigid	Loss of memory, absence of desire
Po	Metal	Internalization	Obsession with future, neurotic	Vulnerable, total disinterest in life
Zhi	Water	Will to survive, accumulation	Authoritative, dominating	No will, indecisive fear
Hun	Wood	Externalization personality	Defensive	Low self-esteem

Though each of the Five Shen corresponds to a different element and internal organ, the totality of the Five Shen is directed by the heart. All of the Shen sit in the heart because the heart is the real link between divine energy and human energy.

The Five Shen

ELEMENT	ORGAN	NAME OF SHEN
Fire	Heart	Shen
Earth	Spleen	Yi
Air/Metal	Lungs	Po
Water	Kidney	Zhi
Wood	Liver	Hun

SHEN
FIRE-HEART *Governs Emotion.* It is not the heart itself that governs emotion, but the Shen, the spirit, of the heart. If it were the heart, then all emotion would be "burned."

YI
SPLEEN-EARTH *Governs Reflection and Thinking*

PO
LUNGS-AIR *Governs the movement of Internalization.* The work of internalization of energy and emotion is done by PO. The quality of this Shen explains why we keep inside, or internalize, sadness in the lungs. There could not be sadness in the heart, for the heart would burn it. But the quality of PO is internalization. Thus, the emotion which corresponds to the lungs, sadness, will stay inside of the lungs.

ZHI
KIDNEYS-WATER *Governs the Will and the Instinct of Reproduction*

HUN
LIVER-WOOD *Governs Externalization*

Sound and Acupuncture

YANG   FIRE associated with systems of distribution: yang of yang.
WOOD associated with systems of externalization: yang of yin

YIN   METAL associated with systems of accumulation: yin of yang.
WATER associated with systems of internalization: yin of yin.

Explanation of the Chinese Shen Ideograms

Influence from Sky: Influence from Earth:

The square of the ideogram = earth

- Cosmic understanding
- Celestial spirit
- Conscious life
- Sun

- Earthly understanding
- Terrestrial spirit
- Vegetative life
- Link with matter
- Organs that belong to the vegetative system - that is, organs that do not move by themselves.

Etymology of the Ideogram in Two Parts

Part One: Cosmic energy comes from the sky and teaches the human being. From this perspective, we receive the idea of things being superior, coming "from above": the sun, the moon, the stars. The activity of these celestial bodies reveals to humanity all things transcendental.

Part Two: The second part of the ideogram, the earth influence, shows two hands which are tensing a string. This image symbolizes the idea of expansion of movement, stretching toward infinity.

The element aspect of the Shen brings the energy from the cosmos while the organ aspect is linked with earth, the human body, the blood and the direction south.

The spiritual part of the Shen, depicted by the ideogram on the left, brings the cosmic energy to the earth energy. The spiritual Shen is called the Original Shen. It is linked with Yuan Chi, the original chi. This original chi carries the ancestral energy and is connected with the three chi of the anterior sky, the Innate Chi. [6]

The organic Shen, the earth shen, sits in the heart from gestation. It is activated at birth and never ceases its gathering of information and its own pursuit of self-awareness.

On the dynamic level, the Shen represents the expansion, the integration, the psychic circulation of information, a function which likens the Shen to the subtle bodies. In other words, it represents the way we behave in the universe around us. Whether manifested or not, the Shen represent the Principles of Life. The Shen are linked with the organic level in Chinese Medicine. They represent a type of subtle energy system between the chakras and the subtle bodies. This subtle energy system is structured so that each Shen is linked with an internal organ.

The Shen disappear at the moment of death to return to the sky, bringing with them the acquisition of the consciousness in the incarnation. Shen are indestructible and not limited by time in their essence. The Principles of Life which the Shen represent, describe the insertion of the spiritual into time. In this way the Shen are associated with the Ancestral Chi, the Innate Chi and the Acquired Chi.[7]

Sound and Acupuncture

The Qualities of Each of the Five Shen

*The Shen of the Heart
Linked with Fire*

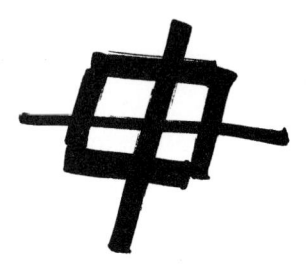

• Controller of the Shen   • Balance

Joy is associated with the Shen of the Heart. The joy in life must be in balance; lack of joy or too much joy both imbalance the heart energies.

The conflict between the Shen and society - between each human being and his or her environment - affects the heart and creates imbalance. This internal conflict might be sublimated into constant laughing or mental over-excitation if too much energy in the Shen has created an imbalance. Inversely, exhaustion, timidity or continual complaining indicates lack of energy in the Shen. In either case there is a need to reharmonize the Shen in order to return to natural emotional behavior and to discern the underlying unity of life.

*The Yi of the Spleen
Linked with Earth*

* Linked with the tongue
* Linked with sound
* Linked with speech
* The realization of the synthesis of existence

The ideogram of the spleen represents the tongue - the intention behind the sound we produce. It symbolizes the vibratory root of human nature.

The Yi is right thinking. It is the intention we put in sound in connection with love and the creative word. The central position of the earth element in the Five Element Cycle has the value of the Christ Logos or the Word, implying that the word has the power to create.

The ideogram depicts a man standing on the earth who speaks to exalt his fruit: his power to speak and create with his words. He speaks in a harmonious, musical way. The music is, above all, the music of the sky, the music of the heart, pure inspiration linked from the center of his being through his central axis to the sky. The Yi represents a "right" or true vibration.

The purpose of the Yi is to realize the synthesis of existence. It is universal, innate memory. By its position, it puts us in relationship with the manifested and nonmanifested world. The Yi contains the fusion of the target with the arrow in its center, the fusion of the lover and the beloved in ourselves.

The Yi, through its double polarity, constitutes the world of the creative idea and the world of reflective thinking. In the movement of the Yi there is unified internalization and externalization. The center performs the role of regulation and harmonization (as does the spleen in the body). The Yi is our paradigm of the world - how we act in the world, knowing that the world is, in reality, a reflection of ourselves.

Excess of spleen energy linked with the Yi leads to repetition, obsessing over the past, rigid thinking, and feeling thick and heavy. Lack of energy in the spleen leads to forgetfulness, loss of memory, anxiety, stress and the absence of desire.

*The Po of the Lungs
Linked with Metal*

• Soul incarnated in the body   • Structure of the body

The Po is Yin. It concerns the creation of form. Its ideogram is "The soul which resides in the body." The Po is the Principle of Structure in the body. It encourages us to bring into reflection everything that is useful to us.

The Po is the cellular instinct. It is the "I am, "I exist." It is the vital instinct of the species. The Po contains hereditary memory (through the prana) and offers an energy to the will of the Zhi, the Shen of the kidneys, linked with water. The Po, in realizing form, offers this energy to the Zhi which will then act on it.

The Po is pure realization. As the Hun is consciousness, the Po is unconsciousness.

When there is excess fullness of Po in the lungs, there is also an obsession directed toward the future (the obsession of the Yang-Ming).[8] We can also experience sadness and dread with accompanying sighing and complaining and a tendency toward more and more internalization.

When the Po is empty, the instinct of conservation becomes lost. We become very vulnerable and disinterested in life and cry often. We also experience sorrow and worry which comes from the imbalance of the energy of the lungs (as is the case for people who awaken at 3:00 a.m. and lay awake the rest of the night worrying).

Sound and Acupuncture

*The Zhi of the Kidney
Linked with Water*

志

- Idea of development
- Deep aspirations

The Zhi is Yin, and corresponds to the accumulation of energy. Its ideogram represents the idea of development, moving toward a fixed goal. Linked with the kidneys and water, the Zhi underlies the growing aspiration, the deep *elan* toward manifestation, power, the will to live and procreate, the "I want." The Po says "I exist," but the Zhi says "I want."

The Zhi assures, with the help of the earth, the realization of the dense body. It represents sexuality in the sense of the instinct to reproduce, the desire of realization. The role of the Zhi is to preserve form, to support integration and accumulation.

If external information is too overwhelming, the balance of the Zhi is lost and we experience fear, which pulls us to a lower energetic level in the Zhi's system of distribution of chi. Fear produces the lessening of activity in the world, of contact with the outside.

Fullness of energy in the kidneys leads to an excess of will, volunteerism, temerity and authoritarianism. Lack of energy in the kidneys produces indecision, visceral fear, sexual problems such as impotence and sterility, and lowers the will.

There can be two origins of the fear associated with an imbalance of the Zhi:

1. Emotional fear linked with the solar plexus.
2. Visceral fear linked with the kidneys. This instinctive fear is with or without reason such as fear of the dark, of death, of the absurd or of all that could destroy the shape or form in life.

The Hun of the Liver
Linked with Wood

- Cosmic aspect
- Shape of the moon
- Clouds rolling in the sky

- The nature of strength and power
- Linked with earth

The Hun is yang, associated with spring. It seems to be exalted by the heart (like a wood tree). It is associated with the birth of the yang and its movement creates a link with the sun. It erupts from the earth like the sap rising in a tree.

The Hun is a part of the luminous spirit. Its destiny is to go out of the eternal night and to enter the luminous sky - the world of light. Linked with the earth, it brings to us all that touches the heritage of the past. Perhaps this function connects us during dreams to the great archetypes and symbols of the universe.

The liver realizes the transformation of the shape (earth) from the non-I to the I. (The elements absorbed at the level of digestion are transformed by the liver.) The Hun is the consciousness of the I, the personality, and represents the acquisition of consciousness through imagery. It has the capacity to think in images, to suggest to the mind images that are appropriate to the situation. The Hun also symbolizes the movement of going forward. The impulsive energy of the wood gives us the capacity to create an image which permits us to go beyond the illusory world.

The Hun is also linked with the energy of defense, the role of the gall bladder. This defense is applied to the consciousness of the I - whether the defense is located in the mind or in the immune system.

The Will and the Five Shen

Whenever one of the internal organs is associated with stubbornness, overbearing will or the unwillingness to let go when appropriate there will be an interior excess of the corresponding Shen quality. For example:

When the liver is associated with an overbearing will, an overflow of anger is produced.
The heart in association with an overbearing will, results in an excess of joy.
When the spleen is associated with an overbearing will, preoccupation becomes excessive.
When the lungs are associated with an overbearing will, sadness predominates.
When the kidneys are associated with an overbearing will, excess fear is produced.

It is the Shen, through their specific relationship with the elements of nature, that can transmit energy and spirit to the internal organs. The Shen enable us to link internal organs to the elements. Work in nature, practice with chi movement, acoustic music or healing with such vibrational tools as sound and color help to open the Shen and produce harmony between the earth and sky energies in our bodies.

Musical Link, Earth to Sky:
Acoustic Instruments, the Five Elements and the Five Shen

The pure sound of acoustic instruments resonates with the human body because these instruments are made of the five elements of nature and the Shen. The vibrational essence wood, for example, is carried through the sound of the wood flute. There is a resonance with this sound in the body through the wood of the liver and gall bladder. The natural overtones produced by the wood flute will reach the subtle body energy of its own Shen, the spiritual "wood", the Hun.[9] There are musical instruments for each of the five elements which all help to balance our organs and the corresponding Shen.[10]

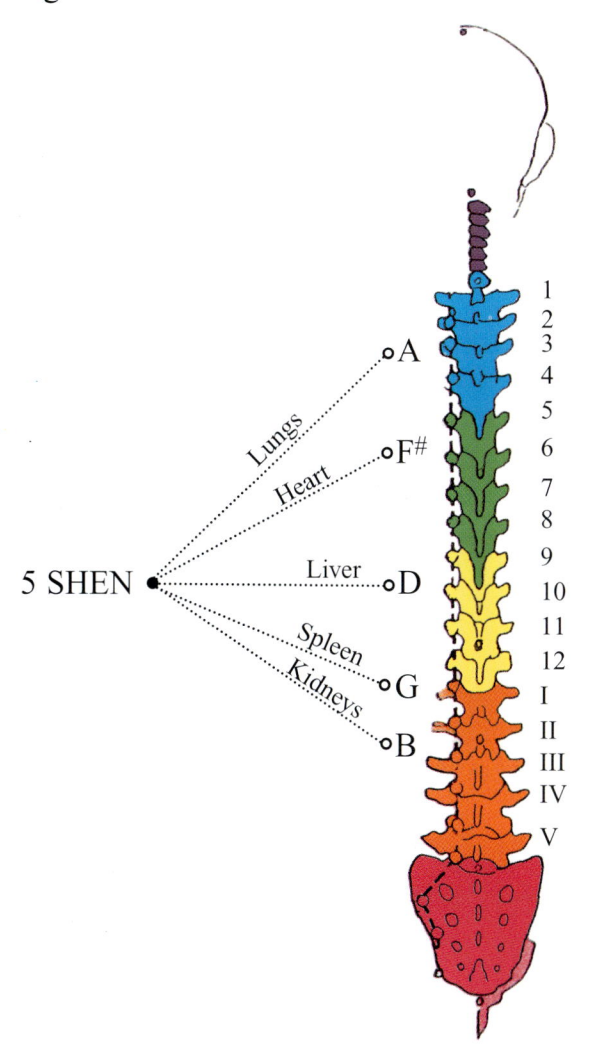

5 SHEN
- Lungs — A
- Heart — F#
- Liver — D
- Spleen — G
- Kidneys — B

(Book IV of this series, *Healing with Sound, Color and Movement* offers several techniques such as "The Musical Spine", which utilizes the correspondence between music, the five elements and the physical and subtle bodies).

Chapter Three

Organic Psychology: The Psychology of the Temperaments

As we have seen, the five elements of nature form the essence of our physical anatomy through their correspondence with the internal organs of the body. The different qualities of the five elements all work together in unique combinations to form the biological temperament of each human being. From this biological makeup, our psychological temperament is formed. Through the Law of the Five Elements, Chinese Oriental Medicine offers a link to biology which would give individual psychological and emotional traits an organic base in the physical body.

The practice of Western psychotherapy has made much progress in the past one hundred years, yet how healthy psychologically have we really become as a result? Families, in particular, seem to suffer as the critical eye of psychotherapy can point out every detail of dysfunction, but do very little to repair the damage. When psychotherapy, or any discipline, is severed from its organic resonance in nature or the human body, the results become mental paradigms which may become popular for a time but have no lasting resonance with real human "nature."

Through an understanding of the six basic temperaments in Chinese Medicine, we have a window into the psychological roots of our own nature and into that of our partners in life. For example, when a flash of anger is understood as a liver complication, or as a fire-wood imbalance, we release some of our personal defensiveness and reactions and can find help in the larger patterns of nature. A flash of fire burns wood and then just as quickly dies when the fuel, wood, is gone. If we are forced to process the anger psychologically, feeding it further with explanations, analysis, or long searches into historical causes, this anger can hurt others or live longer than its original spontaneous outburst needed to rebalance internal organ energies.

The Six Temperaments

A psychological temperament is formed by the association of two elements. The two elements create an organic base which can help in the diagnosis of physical or psychological problems. There are six basic temperaments, three Yang and three Yin.[11]

The Three Yang Aspects

SHAO YANG		TAE YANG		YANG MING	
wood	*fire*	*water*	*fire*	*earth*	*metal*
Gall Bladder	Triple Warmer	Bladder	Small Intestine	Stomach	Large Intestine

The Three Yin Aspects

TSUE YIN		SHAO YIN		TAE YIN	
wood	*fire*	*water*	*fire*	*earth*	*metal*
Liver	Pericardium	Kidneys	Heart	Spleen	Lungs

Each temperament is composed by the association of two elements representing two Yang organs or two Yin organs. In Chinese Medicine the Six Temperaments are called the Six Entities which represent the qualities of the sky. A person's temperament is determined at birth according to the quality of energy one brings into incarnation. This birth energy is discerned by taking into account the quality of energy of the year (shown in the chart in the Appendix on page 125), the season, the hour of birth and the heredity of the chi running in the organ which corresponds to the hour of birth. For example, if you are born with a strong stomach and large intestine, you will have a Yang Ming temperament while the other qualities of energy will be less pronounced.

Accepting that our different ways of being in the world have clear biological roots and express the elements of nature can do much to promote interpersonal and even international tolerance and understanding. While each person reflects a unique integration of qualities of all of the six temperaments, there is usually one particular temperament which influences the basic psychological structure. In the following chart and explanations, each temperament will be described by its typical emotional and mental tendencies.

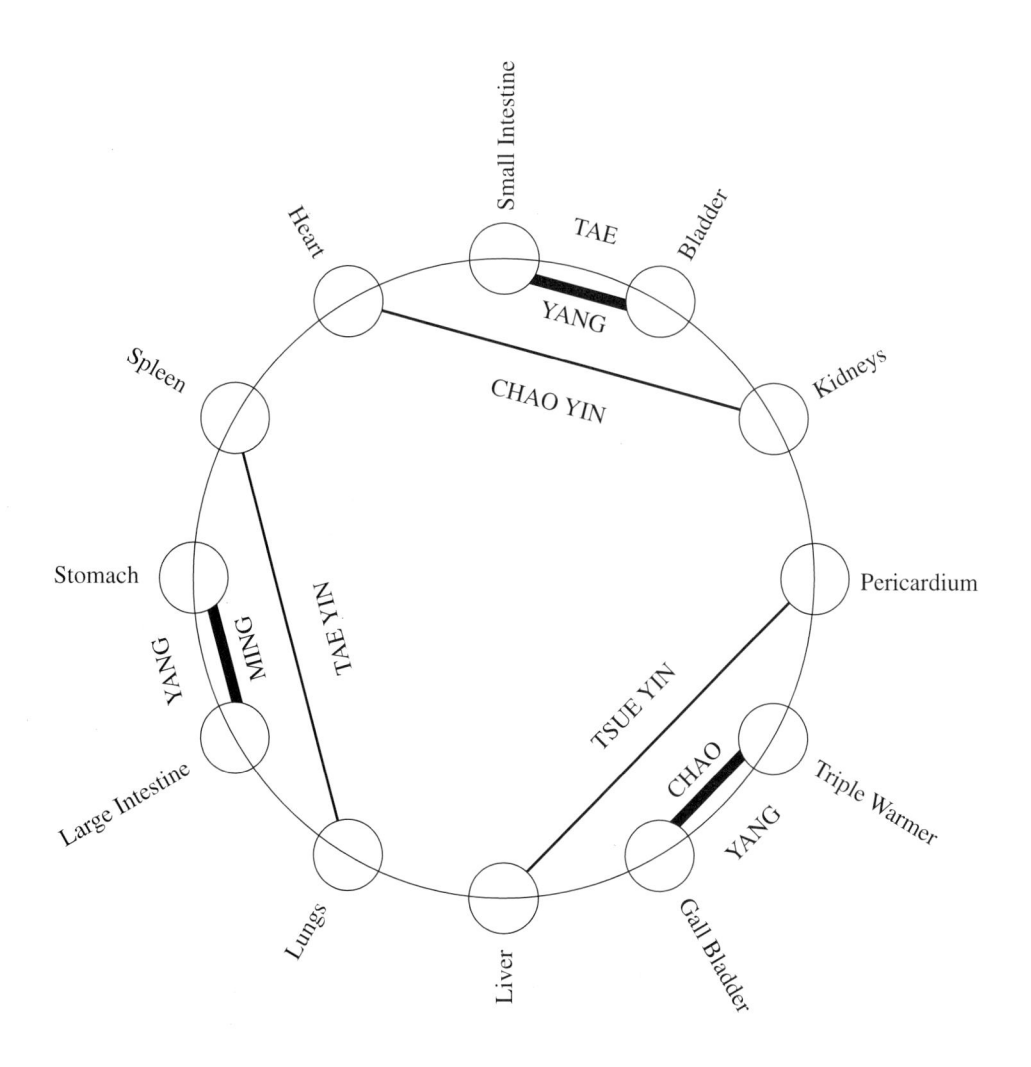

The Relationship Among The Six Entities

SHAO YANG QUALITIES
Gall Bladder, Triple Warmer

EMOTIVE

Quick-tempered
Angry, irritable, explosive (for short periods, but often)
Aggressivity alternates with depression
Not vindictive
Express themselves easily
Can be emotive for no apparent reason (Triple Warmer energies)

ACTIVE

Hyperactive, restless, agitated
Cannot stay in one place or sit and be quiet
Must move or exercise, like to walk all the time
Not afraid to work, do all kinds of things
Balanced and fast, quick reactions
Extremely energetic, electric
Superficial energy (capillaries)
Diffused energy, likes to go in many directions

SPONTANEOUS

No inhibition, complete expansion
Impulsive, impatient

PHYSICAL CHARACTERISTICS

Large shoulders
Bushy sideburns, thick beard, and hairy (means more blood than energy)
Large orbital cavities or eye sockets (means gall bladder strong)
Eyes pop out (means gall bladder meridian too full)
Eyes sink in (means gall bladder meridian empty)
Spine of nose is high

IN GENERAL

Noble, like a Spanish Toreador
Expressive and quick-tempered like John McEnroe
Pretentious and showy
Think they can do everything themselves
Generous
Optimistic
Full of vitality, exuberant
No moderation or suppression of reaction
Link everything: politics, people, progress
Revolutionary
Go in many directions
Need to give their advice, opinion, ("Big Gall Bladder")
Like to control, direct, command, organize
Difficult to deal with
Not forgetful
Learn from mistakes, but slowly
Healthy libido
Not weakened by conflicts with others, use conflicts as opportunity to express their strength and power
Heaviness in the morning, hard to get out of bed
Euphoric in evening, building to the time when the energy is in the gall bladder, 11:00 p.m.
People from the Mediterranean region are often Shao Yang.

TSUE YIN QUALITIES
Liver, Pericardium

EMOTIVE

Nervous tempered
Interior emotivity
Inhibition of emotivity
Difficult to express emotions - they stay stuck inside
Have many thoughts and ideas which they cannot express
Keep everything inside

Cannot live with outer "reality" so create their own inner reality
Escape into imagination into myths and symbols
Can also escape with drugs, "artificial paradise," tobacco or superficial games
Need stimulants, not only chemical, but also emotional and intellectual
Contradictory
Live in present with idea of past
Feel any conflict heavily on shoulders, each conflict is felt as if it is the end of the world
Often agitated
If too repressed, they become aggressive, even violent
Unstable
Swear and insult if angry
Hypersensitive
Afraid of emptiness
Claustrophobic
Agoraphobic
Afraid of needles (in acupuncture)
Afraid of any sudden noise, jumpy
Intolerance to wind or high altitudes
Intolerance to alcohol

NON-ACTIVE

Will not act without strong motivation
Not a "real worker"
Irregular worker, makes intermittent effort
Once they act, however, can achieve a tremendous amount of work
Results of effort more brilliant than solid
After strong activity with deep motivation and enormous work, become depressed, nervous, irritable
Have times of activity and times of non-activity (activity/emptiness)
Nervous, agitated

PHYSICAL CHARACTERISTICS

Complexion is generally rose colored, rose is congested when not in good health. In poor health, color is pale and empty

If eyes are more or less big, it means liver is more or less strong

Have more blood than energy

IN GENERAL

Have good taste, enjoy simple beauties like the French people do
Fine energetic presence
Mystical energy
Creative, imaginative
Detect sensitive things
Gentle
Can go into confusion easily, in extreme cases complete delirium
Sometimes cannot remember what they are doing
Loss of memory if blood goes down and energy goes up
Dizziness if blood goes up and energy goes down
Perspire profusely, specifically hands, feet and forehead
A Tsue Yin person may choose to be a poet or to work in the fashion industry.

YANG MING EARTH QUALITIES
(Stomach, Large Intestine)

NON-EMOTIVE

Cold mind
Objective
Can be like a robot
Difficult to move from position because they don't feel the conflict
Do not put responsibility of conflicts on their shoulders
Do not tend to feel anything weighing heavily on themselves

Not disturbed by emotion or lack of emotion
Love affairs are never tragic for them
Are not passionate or emotional in love, pleasure, sports
Do not ask themselves if they "feel like this or that"
Maturation of ideas happens internally
Easy to live with, easy to deal with
Have a natural joy (but when unbalanced or in excess joy could become manic euphoria)
Can have a very terrible anger if unbalanced (because they are very strong people)
Groan a lot and become very irritable if unbalanced
Possibility of shallow development because of non-emotivity
Generally never ill

ACTIVE

More extroverted than Yang Ming Metal
Strong people because yin and yang are balanced
Can dominate and be active in a paralyzing, emotionally disturbing situation
Can lead
Can organize huge events involving thousands of people
Total success in everything they do (no inhibition of emotion to retard success)
Prefer experiencing life to thinking about it
Talented with their hands
Love practical things, practical activities and practical intelligence
Do many things, very active in the world without being affected by others
Can do any type of activity, not looking for honor
Not ambitious in their activity
Can eat large amounts or food without being affected

PHYSICAL CHARACTERISTICS

When blood and energy is balanced, they have strong neck, large chest and very solid stomach

IN GENERAL

Both primary and secondary in their actions, reactions
Yin and yang in perfect balance when in good health
The blood and energy are perfectly equal when in good health
Constitution and mentality in perfect balance when in good health
Polite
Generous
Kindly
Reserved
Impression of total harmony
Quiet
Level-headed
Tactful, diplomatic
Tolerant
Exact, meticulous observation and skills (if unbalanced they become obsessive over details)
Remarkable practical sense
Very smart
Ironical
Spiritual
Organized, clear mind for organizing
Controller
Do not like abstractions, theory or speculation
Do not like big complicated systems like bureaucracies
Not attached to the law, know how to exploit the law and use it for themselves
Subtlety of mind
Understand very quickly
Clever
Adapt themselves very quickly
Opportunists

YANG MING METAL
(Large Intestine, Stomach)

NON-EMOTIVE

Cold mind
Objective observation
Rarely "turned upside down" by outside influences, ideas, people
Inflexible, stubborn
Strict
Stoic (showing austere indifference to joy, grief, pleasure or pain; calm and unflinching when suffering)
Quiet
Distant
Impassive, not showing emotion - placid, serene
Phlegmatic - having a temperament not easily disconcerted or aroused
Laconic attitude
Brief or terse in speech or expression
Make the best judges because of emotionless objectivity
Live by "the Law is the Law," strong principles
Good sense of humor
Love story summarized as "If you stay, ok. If not, there are always more fish in the sea"

ACTIVE

Phlegmatic, hard to rouse to action, sluggish, dull, apathetic
Calm, cool, solid
Unexcitable, showing no sensitivity
Deep civic sense
Patrol like a policemen, telling people not to do this or that
Meticulous (taken to an extreme becomes sadistic)
Orderly
Manipulative

RESTRAINED

The past will not only reinforce the present, it will determine the present
Can be primary or secondary in their actions/reactions
Can have an immediate answer or a late answer

PHYSICAL CHARACTERISTICS

Have lots of blood and lots of energy
Long neck
Long waisted
Solid stomach
If nose is large, then large intestine is strong
If they have big beards and fleshy faces, they have more blood than energy
Complexion will be rosy

IN GENERAL

Principled
Simple
Level-headed
Tactful, diplomatic
Very moral
Their religion will have a moral aspect intended to bring social order
Like abstract systems, theory, speculation
Brilliant manipulation of concepts in an abstract system
Clairvoyant in sensing character

TAE YIN EARTH
(Spleen, Lungs)

NON-EMOTIVE

Quiet
Tolerant through indifference
Indifferent to past and future
Thick-skinned, resistant

Carry old sadness
When in balance, they are happy, carefree, unconcerned
Light
Detached, do not feel the pressure of conflict
Can eat a lot

NON-ACTIVE

Not ambitious
Persisting through passivity and stubbornness
Like music (especially Mozart) and theater
Can be composers or actors
Non-punctual
Lazy
Cyclical patterns of difficulty waking up
Can bend but never break, like bamboo
Inertia is their strength (inertia is stronger than physical strength because inertia has no limit)
Appear to give up in conflict, but are just waiting for the storm to pass
Old sadness stops them from acting
Blind to opportunities around them; could die in one spot even if the help they needed was right next to them

SPONTANEOUS

Give in to any impulse
Like pleasure
Change with the wind (not excited about change, just go with the flow; if there is no wind, they do not move or change)
Feel lightness inversely proportional to their weight

PHYSICAL CHARACTERISTICS

Complexion will be yellow
Big, round face, full cheeks

Thick fleshly back and shoulders
Large legs and belly, not muscular
Small hands and feet
Could be quite heavy if they eat often

IN GENERAL

Look happy as if the sun is in their eyes
Generous
Tolerant
Do not like too much honor bestowed upon them
Rational
Orderly

TAE YIN METAL
(Lungs, Spleen)

NON-EMOTIVE

Apathetic
Stoic
Metal characteristics of grief, sadness, weeping
Emotionally cold
Respond to questions like a recorder - yes, no
Simple
Indifferent
Unconcerned
Closed
Secretive
Quiet
Rarely laugh
Vindictive
Hold a deep sadness
Introverted
Obsessive with a meticulous aspect
Excessively scrupulous

NON-ACTIVE

Sly
Perfidious (treacherous but without physical power)
Falsely polite
Fearful (because they have no yang)
Taciturn (almost always silent, uncommunicative)
Sad quietness, sad silence
Like not to be seen
Passive
Very slow physically and mentally
Limited mentally because of difficulty in focusing, concentrating
Difficulty staying "on track"
Speak slowly in monotone
Tire quickly in any effort
Eat slowly
Total inertia is their power because inertia can inhibit all activity around them
Economize movement which leads to habits of economy
Strong power of meditation, can sit forever
No yang power to mobilize themselves for action
Passive, non-reactive
Meticulous

RESTRAINED

Quiet
Turned inward, but without exciting inner life
Profound introversion
Inertia their master
Cold

PHYSICAL CHARACTERISTICS

Long body, specifically femur bone
White, pale complexion when not healthy

Little head, shoulder, hands, feet
Blonde hair, blue eyes typical
Small stomach, big intestine
Thin skin
Can take drugs
Can die young

IN GENERAL

Generally honest and honorable
Gifted with deep inner knowledge

SHAO YIN
(Heart, Kidney)

EMOTIVE

Pretend not to care, but care a lot
Try to appear phlegmatic
Try to hide emotions
Can appear quite cold
Extremely quiet
Meditative (when walking, head is down, hands in back as if meditating on something they cannot express - this cuts energy in head)
Very withdrawn, (others don't feel seen by Shao Yin)
Closed because they feel they will be misunderstood (before talking, they think "oh, what's the use, I won't be understood anyway)
Feel persecuted, misunderstood
Feel explosive, but hold all inside
Fanatical because not able to express their personal sentiment
Fearful, wanting to escape
In conflict with rest of world because so steeped in old culture
Feel conflict of culture, religion
Contradictory

Complicated
Confused
Extremely sensitive
Cry easily
Vulnerable
Intimate
Need intimate situation before they can express
Can be charming - strong sensitive eyes
Taken back by open direct communication if they don't know someone intimately
Sentimental
Modest
Serious
Moral
Scrupulous
Constant
Commitment deeply honored
Envious, enjoys misfortune of others
Can be melancholic if unbalanced
Always faulting themselves
Shy
Ruminate on the past
Not living in present
Difficulties in communicating with others
Feel the absurdities of life
Can be suicidal
If balanced: Strong possibility to transform themselves by establishing deep dialogue with themselves
Self reflective
Strong lucidity of own weaknesses
Ability to transcend all difficulties
Can express genius
Strong will
Joyous
Expressive writers

NON ACTIVE
    Water represses their fire or will-to-express
    Can justify inactivity by saying that is their ideal
    Masters of renunciation
    Inhibited
    Immobile, can sit forever in one place
    Cannot do what they want
    Resignation of inability to advance
    Ambitious, but cannot realize ambitions
    Attitude of retreat
    Wanting to escape
    Disturbed by own ineffective actions
    Old World/New World conflict - desire to modernize but nostalgic about a better past
    Efficient
    Very punctual (important for them)

RESTRAINED
    Introverted
    Non-expressive
    Water represses, finds a way around
    Cannot confront or be direct with actions
    Acts in a round about manner, goes around the point
    Adrenalin low (fight or flight), reason why they don't fight directly.
    Passive-aggresive

PHYSICAL CHARACTERISTICS
    Small stomach, very developed large intestine
    Stomach pulse generally weak
    Bladder and small intestine pulse strong

Blood and energy are weak
Usually have dark circles under eyes
Low adrenalin
Fear linked with low kidney energy
Wet looking eyes, as if about to cry
Often have trouble with heart and vision

IN GENERAL

Feel persecuted
Live with a story of the past

TAE YANG
(Urinary Bladder, Small Intestine)

EMOTIVE

Passionate
Presumptuous
Arrogant
Give orders, command
Obviously proud
Naturally dominate
Like to control self and others
Can be violent (know how to use and control their own violence)
Know how to speak well
Like to be in society
Very serious
Quiet inside
Love stories always dramatic and can be tragic
Suffer because they try to repress emotions
Try to appear indifferent but actually are very passionate

ACTIVE

Very ambitious
Able to realize projects
Able to focus strongly on one idea

Like to serve
Often choose military service
Spirit of sacrifice for an ideal
Can reduce basic needs if necessary
If spouse tries to stop them from achieving their goals, will divorce - no compromise possible
Like hierarchy, need to belong to a group or order
Like to obey orders
Impeccable
Good organizers

RESTRAINED

Inhibited
Move in moderation
Can have cold mind to realize goals

PHYSICAL

Head and back are very straight like military stance

IN GENERAL

Passionate like Russian people
Committed to family, religion, patria
Attached to old values
Have a profound sense of greatness
Could be ascetics
Make good military people
Their challenge is always to choose between expressing or inhibiting their passion.

If you are interested in reading more about the Chinese Temperaments, please refer to the book *Character and Health, The Relationship of Acupuncture and Psychology*, by Yves Requena, published in 1989 by Paradigm Publications, Brookline, MA.

General Treatment Information for the Six Temperaments

When **SHAO YANG** is ill, tonify the yin of the wood and fire and disperse the yang of the wood and fire. If the gall bladder is too full and they exhibit angriness, disperse the yang and stimulate the yin.

When **TSUE YIN** has fullness in the liver, which means the pulse is too tight, they experience anger, hysteria, dizziness and forgetfulness. In this case, disperse the liver and tonify the gall bladder. When Tsue Yin shows emptiness in the liver, they will be anxious and afraid of everything, and will have difficulty seeing and hearing.

Notice that the yang of these fire and wood meridians make up Shao Yang. The yin of the other two fire and wood meridians make up Tsue Yin. If Shao Yang is ill, disperse the energy in the meridians. When Tsue Yin is ill, tonify the energy in the meridians.

For **YANG MING EARTH,** disperse the stomach energy when it is in excess; otherwise they will have cardiovascular problems with the heart. When they become irritable, immediately disperse the stomach energy.

For **YANG MING METAL**, if you see from their forearm that the capillaries are apparent, it means that the large intestine is disturbed. It is very important to look at the forearm when people come for large intestine problems. When the face is hot it means that the stomach is disturbed. The capillaries will be excited and red around ST 42 or ST 41.

The **TAE YIN EARTH** doesn't have much blood or energy, so you must try to balance the energy first, to see where the energy is. NEVER DISPERSE THE YIN, only stimulate the yang. It is difficult to help Tae Yin Earth with only acupuncture.

For **TAE YIN METAL, NEVER DISPERSE THE YIN** - they could die. When you disperse the yin of a typology without fire, these people have no way to recover. If the yin is empty and you disperse the yin by mistake, the Tae Yin Metal has no place to find energy. When fire is in a temperament, the fire energy is always moving like a flame, so the person can always find energy somewhere.

When **TAE YANG** is ill, disperse the yang. Anytime you disperse the yin of the Tae Yang (and especially if, by chance, the yin is empty), madness results! The same madness could result if the yang is too full. Excess of yang leads to madness, but emptiness of the yin can also lead to madness. You must always be careful not to empty the yin.

For the **SHAO YIN**, regulate the energy without dispersing the yin.

Chapter Four

Sound and Acupuncture

Tuning Forks on Meridians

On each acupuncture meridian there are five element points: wood, fire, earth, metal and water. Different orders of the elements appear, depending upon whether the meridian energy is Yin or Yang as shown in the following charts.

Each meridian contains all of the five element points. Each meridian also has a command point which is the point of the same element quality as the meridian itself. For example, the liver corresponds to wood. The liver meridian is a wood meridian. On this wood meridian, the wood point would be the command point.

The heart is fire. On the fire meridian, the command point would be the fire point. Stomach is earth. On the earth meridian, the earth point would be the command point. The lungs are metal. On the metal meridian, the command point would be the metal point. The kidneys are water. On the water meridian, the command point would be the water point.

Tuning forks of different frequencies are applied on the acupuncture command points called Shu, which are the five element points on each of the twelve meridians. This system is also based on a musical system linked with the fundamental note of each meridian.

From the command point we start with the fundamental note of the meridian, building a Cycle of Fifths following the element order on each meridian.

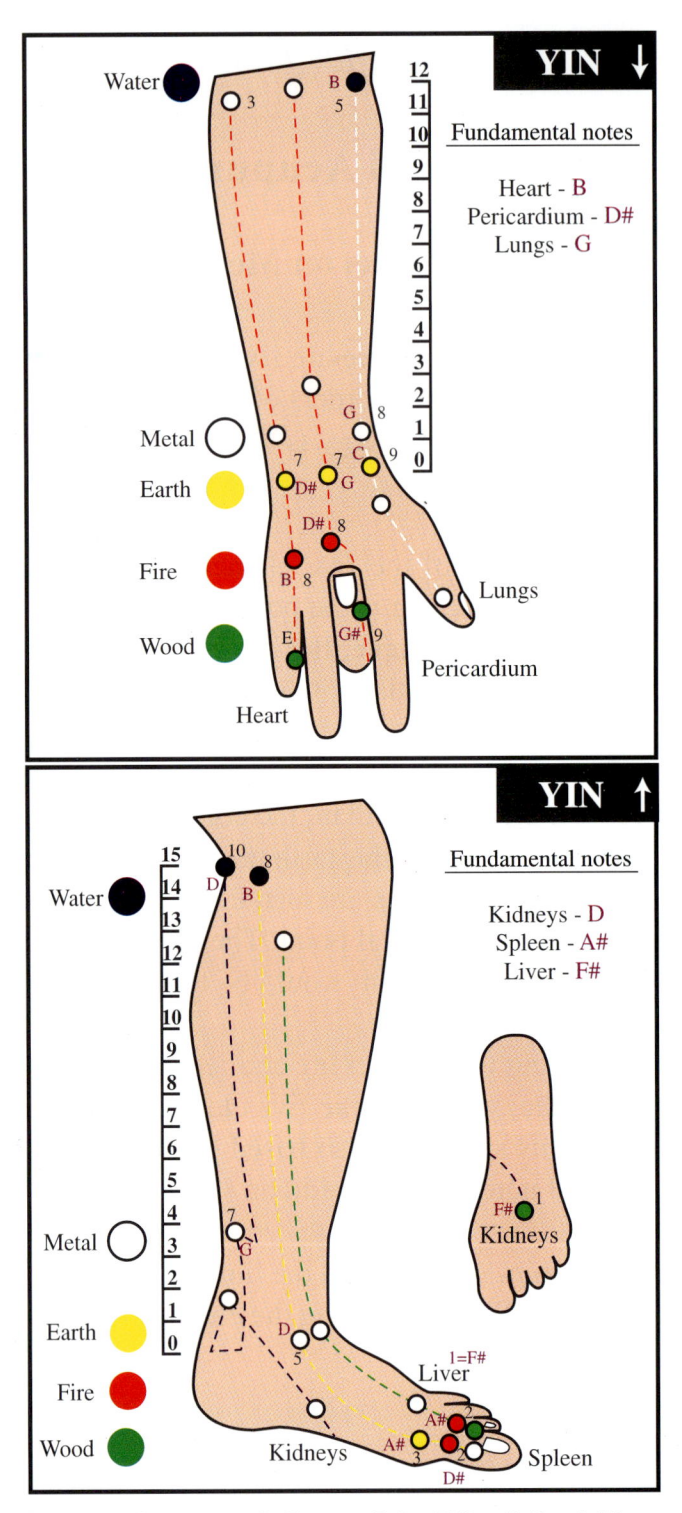

Shu Points and Sound in Yin Meridians

Sound in the Shu Points

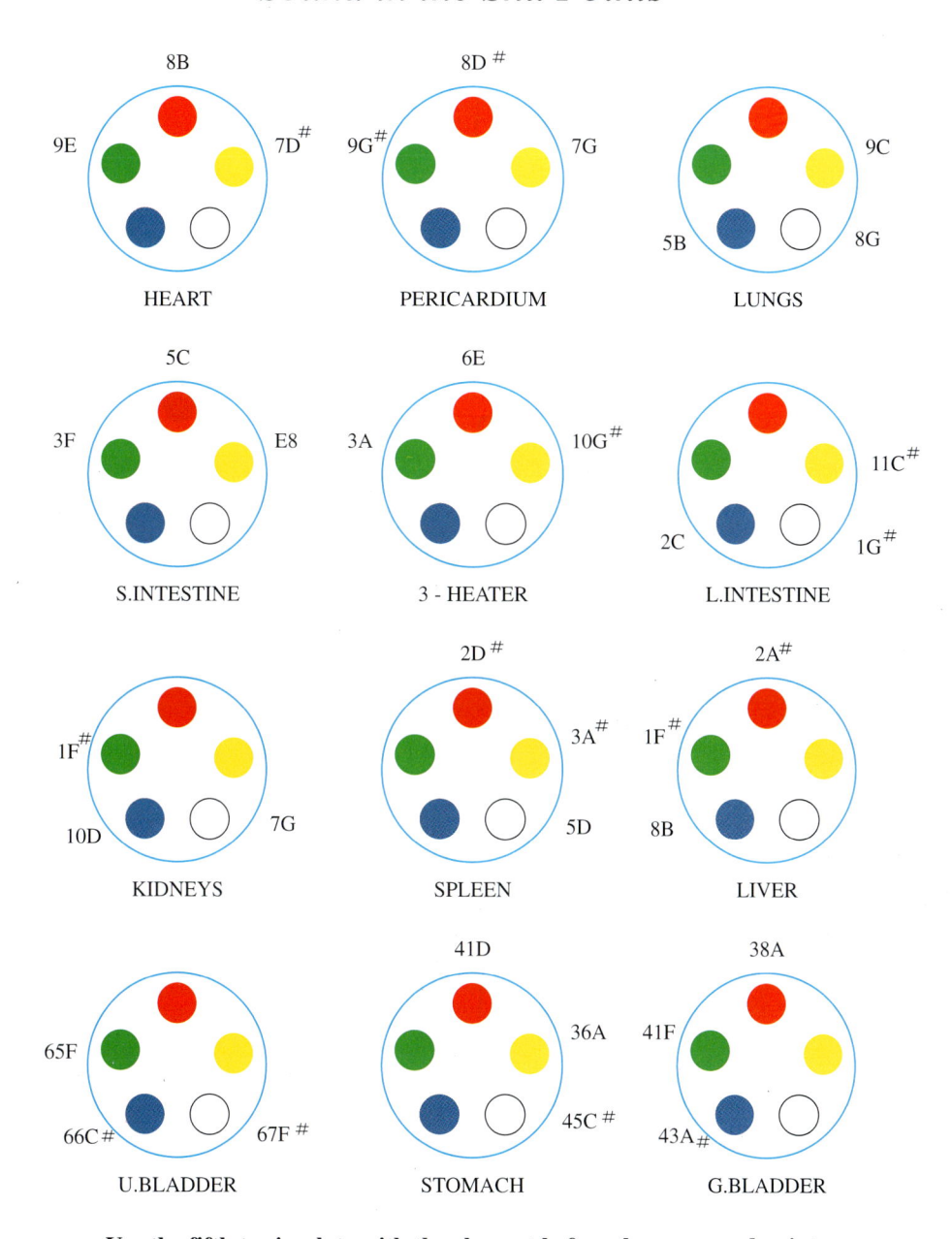

HEART: 8B, 9E, 7D#,

PERICARDIUM: 8D#, 9G#, 7G

LUNGS: (red), 9C, 8G, 5B

S.INTESTINE: 5C, 3F, E8

3-HEATER: 6E, 3A, 10G#

L.INTESTINE: (red), 11C#, 1G#, 2C

KIDNEYS: 1F#, 10D, 7G

SPLEEN: 2D#, 3A#, 5D

LIVER: 2A#, 1F#, 8B

U.BLADDER: 65F, 66C#, 67F#

STOMACH: 41D, 36A, 45C#

G.BLADDER: 38A, 41F, 43A#

Use the fifth to simulate with the element before the command point
Use the third to sedate with the element after the command point

69

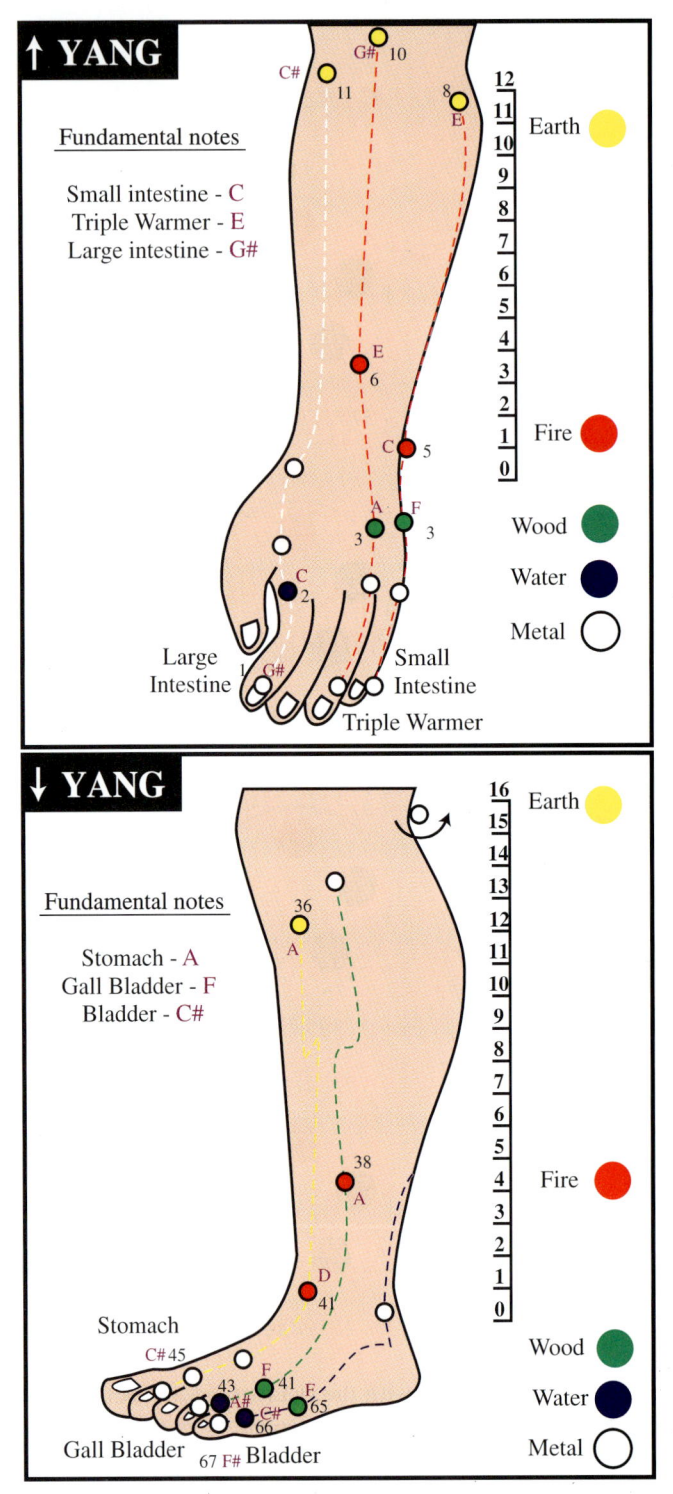

Shu Points and Sound in Yang Meridians

Sound in the Shu Points

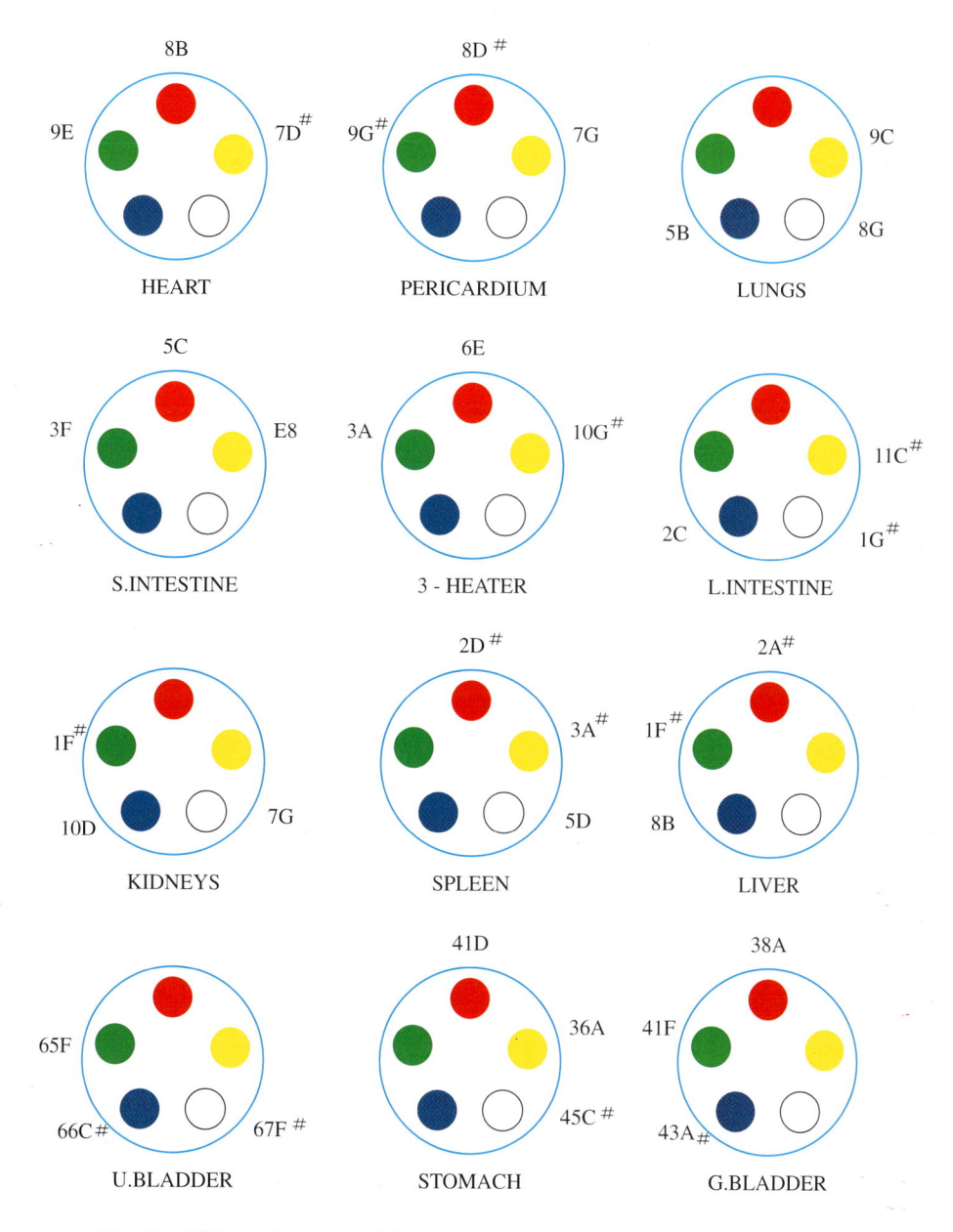

HEART
- 8B
- 9E
- 7D#

PERICARDIUM
- 8D#
- 9G#
- 7G

LUNGS
- 9C
- 5B
- 8G

S.INTESTINE
- 5C
- 3F
- E8

3 - HEATER
- 6E
- 3A
- 10G#

L.INTESTINE
- 11C#
- 2C
- 1G#

KIDNEYS
- 1F#
- 10D
- 7G

SPLEEN
- 2D#
- 3A#
- 5D

LIVER
- 2A#
- 1F#
- 8B

U.BLADDER
- 65F
- 66C#
- 67F#

STOMACH
- 41D
- 36A
- 45C#

G.BLADDER
- 38A
- 41F
- 43A#

Use the fifth to simulate with the element before the command point
Use the third to sedate with the element after the command point

Sound and Acupuncture

Tuning Forks and Shu Points

The fundamental note of each meridian is applied on the command point (the horary point) of the meridian. To move energy along the meridian, we need to create a musical interval between two points. We use the interval of the fifth to stimulate and the interval of the third to sedate the energy in the meridian. We will create a fifth with the element before the command point or a third with the element after the command point, following the Law of the Five Elements.

For example, if you want to stimulate the wood (gall bladder), you would take the tuning fork A# on the water point and F on the wood point. This creates the interval of a fifth finishing on the wood.

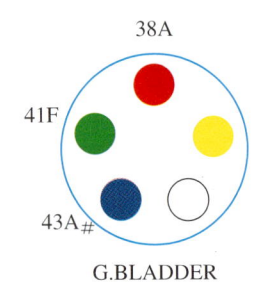

38A

41F

43A#

G.BLADDER

If you want to sedate the wood, use the tuning fork F on the wood point and A on the fire point to create a third. This will sedate or stop the energy of the wood.

In the stimulating sequence you have nourished, or stimulated the wood with water. In the second example you have sedated the wood by using fire, which burns wood. This sequence could stop inflammation of the gall bladder.

The tuning forks used on the acupuncture points act on the physical and etheric level (etheric acupuncture points). The tail of the tuning fork gives the message to the acupuncture point itself and then to the meridian. The fork of the tuning fork vibrates in the etheric body and gives the same message to the etheric energy. When you put a tuning fork on the Shu point it balances the energy because the vibration goes exactly where it is needed. The impulse is given by the vibration of the tuning fork. With the acupuncture needle you send a message to the meridian. The tuning fork works faster because the vibration of sound travels faster than the vibration of the needle.

Because the sound also touches the etheric point, the tuning fork vibration can work to dissolve the crystallization of energy in the etheric as well as in the physical. A perfect resonance is created inside and outside of the body.

This resonance will diminish the adherence of the crystallizations of energy, representing the negative messages which are duplicated from the etheric to the physical body. Ideally, even in acupuncture, we should take care of the subtle bodies in order to eliminate the real source of most physical problems.

In this way the meridian system will be able to balance the energy of the blood and the nervous system. We cannot separate the three systems, meridan, blood and nervous, which interact with each other. When one of these three systems is touched, the other two systems are also modified and balanced.

After using the tuning forks on the meridians, we use the beneficial color of the element on the command point or along the meridian to fix the effect of the sound.

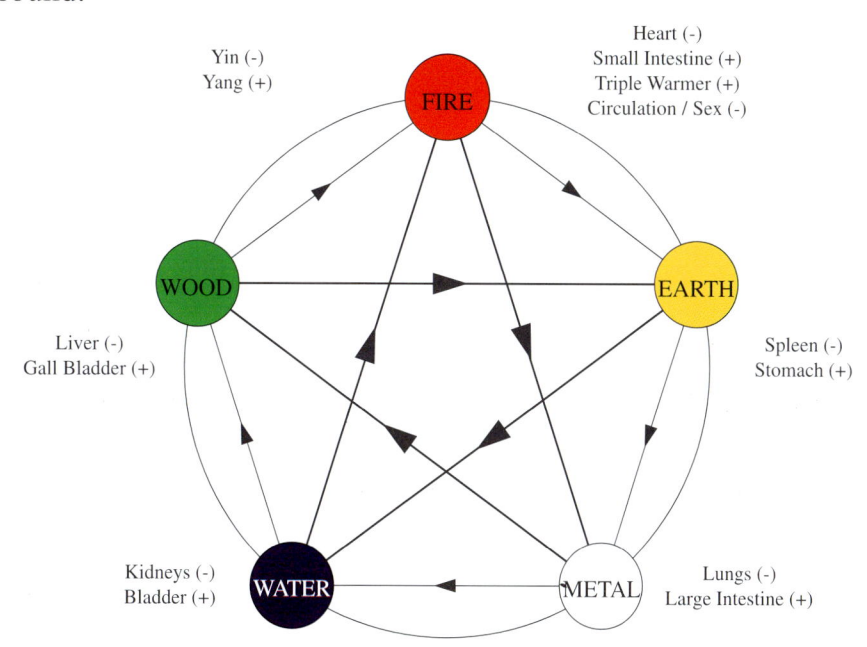

Sound and Acupuncture

When you work with energy, as you listen, you can perceive a quality of vibration which is translated into sound. When acupuncturists insert needles on the meridians, they sometimes hear sound. When inspired, it is possible to hear certain precise musical intervals between points. These sounds, like the acupuncture meridians, always have a resonance with the physical structure, with what we know as the inner structure of the body.

Reprogramming the Cells and the DNA through Sound

Actually, what takes place is that sound works in the subtle bodies to repattern the finer levels of consciousness. This repatterning reaches the physical body through the cyclic resonance or "waves" of the overtones of the sound.

We use this cyclic resonance to reprogram the physical body at the cellular and molecular levels by applying tuning forks to enter the information on certain specific points. In this way, we can reach back through "time" to eight generations of blockages (as implied in the Law of the Eight Elements, or "celestial acupuncture" which is presented in Chapter Six.)

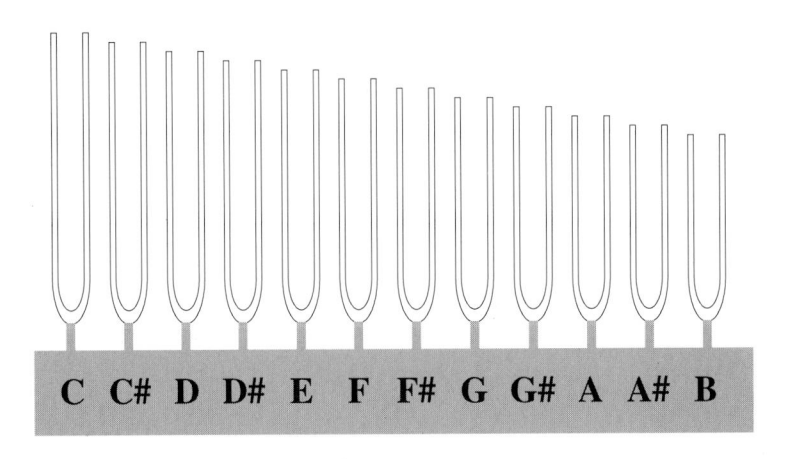

C C# D D# E F F# G G# A A# B

The 12 tuning-forks used for the 12 command points

Function of the Shu Points
Quality of their Musical Intervals

MERIDIAN:					
YANG	metal	water	wood	fire	earth
YIN	wood	fire	earth	metal	water
POINT:	Ting	Rong	Shu	Jung	He
FUNCTION:	attract energy	accelerate energy	absorb energy	penetrate energy	unify energy

The musical interval between two points creates the nature of the movement of the energy.[12] The general nature or quality of each interval is shown in the following chart.

INTERVAL	CREATES
Second	Tension
Third	Sedation
Fourth	Paralysis
Triton (4+)	Division
Fifth	Stimulation
Seventh	Dispersion
Octave	Stillness

The fifth is the most stimulating interval and gives a sense of opening and awareness.

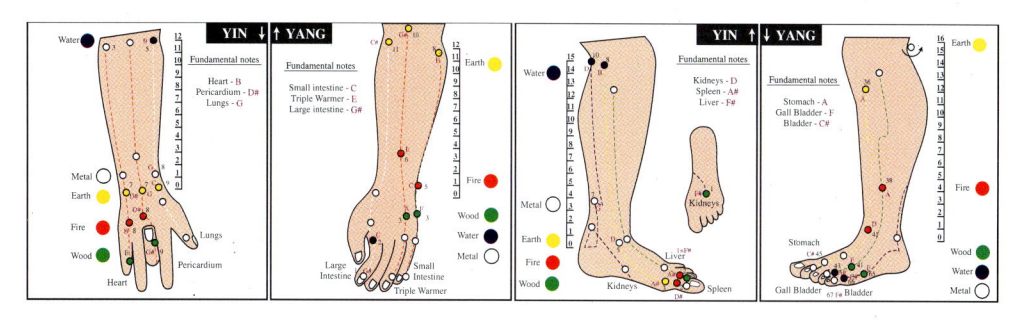

Sound and Acupuncture

The Tuning Fork Technique

To superimpose the musical scale onto the meridian, we move in the direction that the energy flows through the meridian. The scale begins at the tonic (fundamental note) of the meridian and follows the Cycle of Fifths on the successive shu points on the meridian. For example, for the liver meridian, the tonic, F#, is on the wood point, L1. Then, following the Cycle of Fifths in the musical scale (moving up five notes each time), the next point would be C# on the fire point, L2; the G# on the earth point, L3; then D# on the metal point, L4; and A# on the water point, L8.

    F# wood L 1
    C# fire   L 2
    G# earth L 3
    D# metal L 4
    A# water L 8

The liver meridian is Yin. To set up the scale on the Shu Points of the meridian, we followed the Yin order: wood, fire, earth, metal, water.

For the Yang meridians, the Cycle of the Fifths follow the Yang order: earth, fire, wood, water, metal. For example, the Gall Bladder is a Yang meridian:

    F wood   GB 41
    C water GB 43
    G metal GB 44
    D earth GB 34
    A fire   GB 38

The Chinese tradition gives five basic key notes for the five elements. They are as follows:

A - wood - Gall Bladder
G - metal - Lung
F - earth - Stomach
C - fire - Small Intestine
D - water - Kidney

We take into account that there is an inversion between the wood and the earth, when moving from the "little" to the "big" circulation of energy in acupuncture. In the "big circulation", or the Chinese Twenty-Four Hour Clock, the earth becomes A and the wood becomes F. In the "little circulation", or the Law of the Five Elements, the master is the earth as a reference for all the elements.

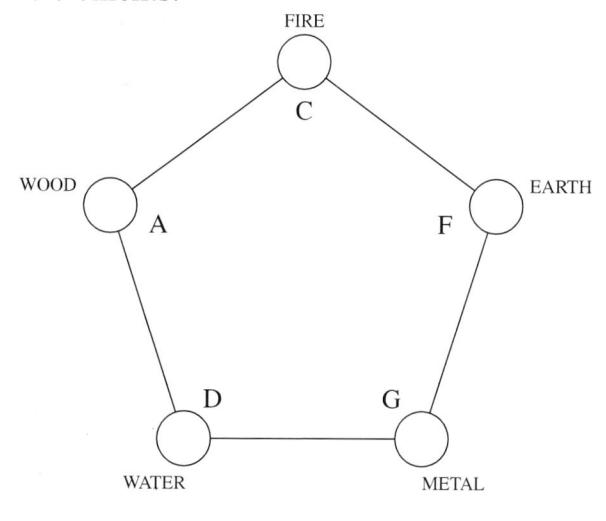

"Little Circulation"
Sheng and Ke Cycles

In the "big circulation", which is the Chinese energetic twenty-four hour clock, the master and reference is the Wood because the Gall Bladder is the decision-maker for all the eleven organs.

For the following chart I simply filled in, from the five basic notes, the schedule for the chromatic tempered scale to find the fundamental note of each meridian.

Sound and Acupuncture

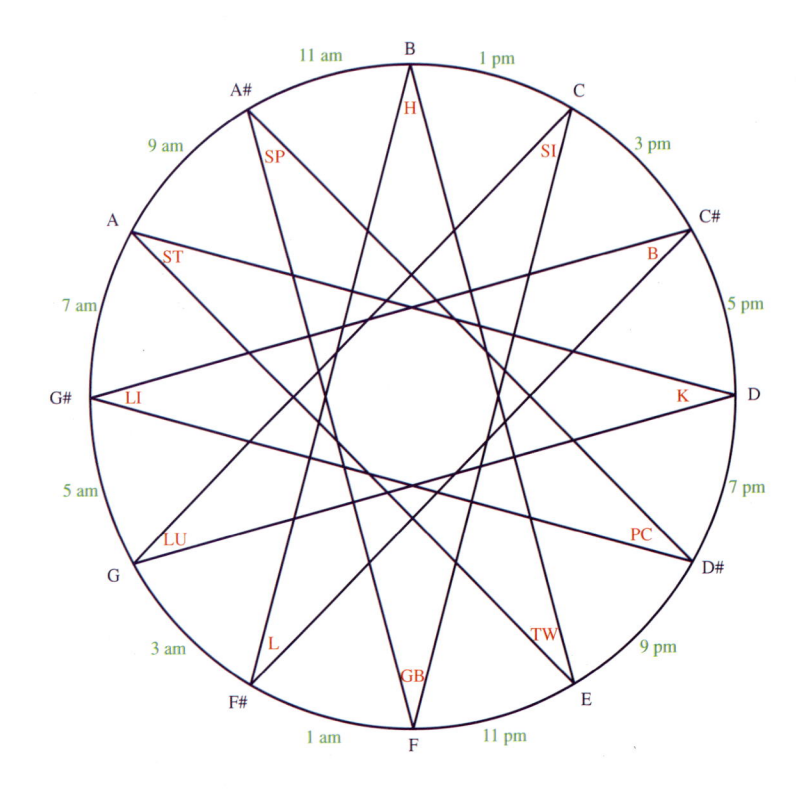

Musical Notes
and
Chinese Twenty-Four Hour Energetic Clock
"The Big Circulation"

In this twenty-four hour energy clock, we superimpose the twelve half tones of the chromatic scale on the disposition of the twelve meridians. The mathematical correspondence of these two systems was too tempting not to try to work with them - and actually it does work. We end with each meridian corresponding to the quality of each note as seen in the chart.

After using the tuning forks on the shu points we use flash lights with optic fiber on the points. Different glass color filters correspond to the beneficial color for the element as given in the five element chart on page 73.

Sound and the Spiral of the Ear

Once while walking on the beach in Exmouth, South England, I picked up a perfectly formed spiral shell. When I put it against my ear to listen to the sound of the sea, I received an insight as to how the ear works. When I held the shell over my ear and turned it slowly around my ear, I heard two different types of musical progressions: first the overtone progression and then the Cycle of Fifths. These musical progressions are described in detail in Book I of this series.

The ear is one of the reflex areas used in acupuncture to represent the entire body. The reflex points of the ear can help release pain quickly. The curve around the lobe of the ear responds to the Cycle of Fifths. If you follow a straight line from any point on the outer lobe to the center of the spiral of the ear, there is the exact progression of overtone as you will see in the charts which follow. So you hear the Cycle of Fifths running along the outer lobe of the ear and the overtone progression going from any point on the outer lobe to the inner parts of the spiral of the ear merging in the central point called "Point Zero" by Dr. Nogier of France.

If you were to superimpose the "sea-shell" composed of the musical notes onto the ear filled with the reflex points, you would find the exact note which corresponds to the part of the body represented by the reflex point. The reflex point would correspond to the note that crosses the straight line running from the outer lobe to the center of the ear.

An interesting observation is that the Point Zero, or 21 (Dr. Nogier), resonates with the frequency A 440. I call Point Zero the "hara of the ear" because it is in the center of the ear. It is easy to understand the importance of the resonance between the center of the ear and the note A 440, which corresponds to the frequency of the spin of electrons.[13] The note A 440 always produced the healing color of pink around human cells in my experiments with sound and cells shown in Book I of this series. Point Zero is used very often to balance the general energy, just as work with the hara can balance energy in the physical body.

Using Tuning Forks on the Ear Points

The magical aspect of sound in the ear, like the sound in the acupuncture meridians, is that the simple act of re-establishing resonance in the point immediately rebalances the energy of the organ or the part of the body that corresponds to the reflex point. What is actually happening is the re-establishment of the free flow of the fluid of the ear through the vibration of the sound. This re-establishes the natural flow of energy all the way back to the source of the imbalance or pain.

When you listen to a sea shell, you hear the perfect resonance of the different arrangements of the sounding lines. If any one of those musical lines were to be interrupted, you would not sense the pleasing spiral of vibration in the shell.

The principle is the same for the ear: When any one point in the ear is not resonating, the entire resonance of the ear is no longer whole. You must re-establish the vibration to return the ear to its natural state, one that sounds like the perfect spiral of vibration of the sea shell.

The diagnosis is made with the R.A.C., "reflex-auriculocardiac" method used by Dr. Nogier of France. Press the points of the ear with a sharp object at the same time that you take the pulse of the wrist. You have two reactions possible:

> A) Pain as the point on the ear is pressed accompanied by a noticeable "jumping" reaction of the pulse. This reaction would indicate an inflammation or a too high concentration of energy.
>
> B) No pain and the pulse disappears. This reaction would indicate a lack of energy.

In both cases, we would apply the tuning fork which corresponds to the frequency of the point to release pain and give the vibrational message to the organ by the meridian. I use very thin tuning forks for the ear, sounding the corresponding frequency on the reflex point according to each zone of the ear as shown in the following ear charts.

The special property of resonance of the tuning fork will work, as on the shu points, to dissolve the crystallization of negative energy (inflammation created by excess energy) in the etheric as well as in the physical body.

Main Points of the Ear

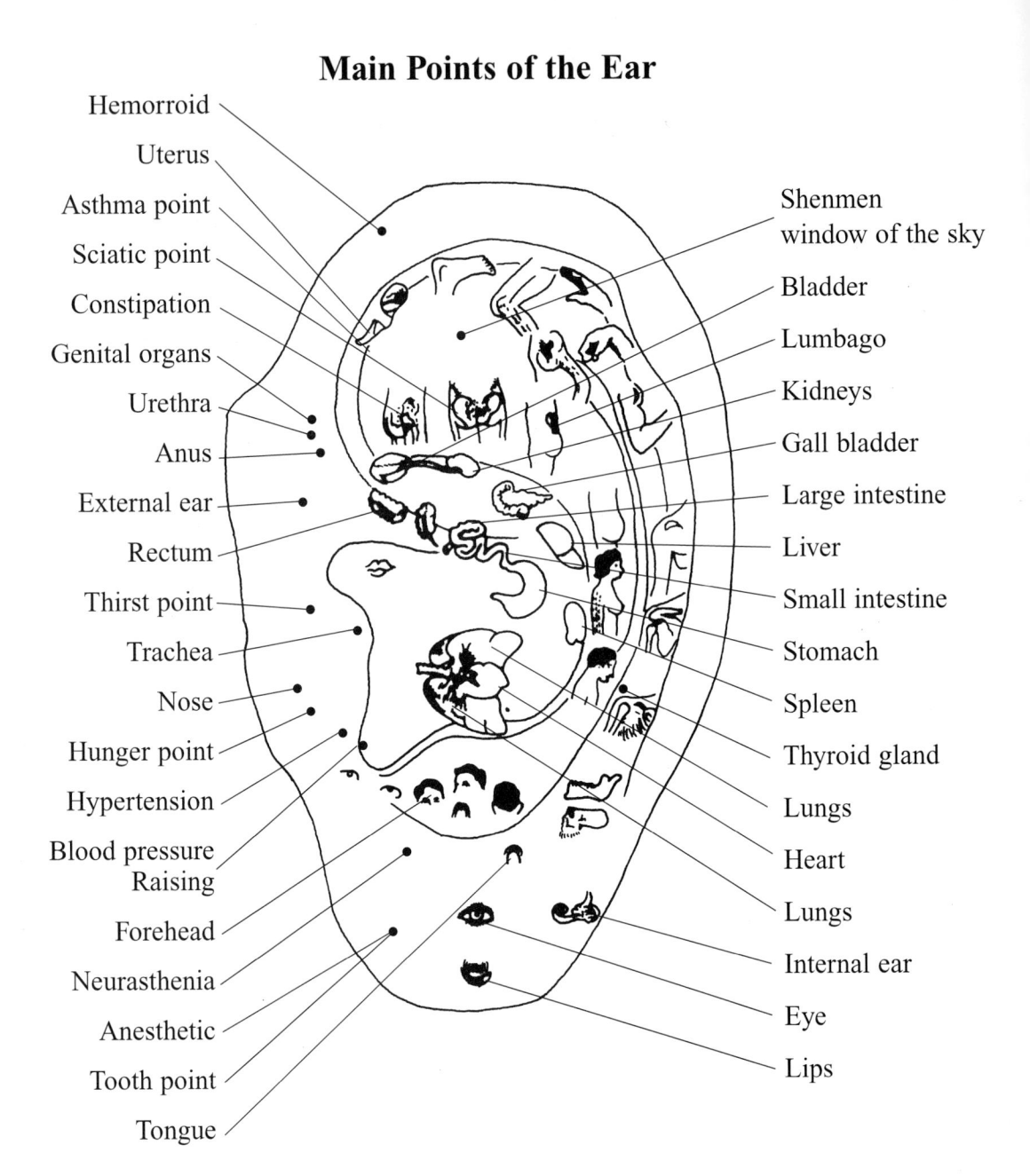

- Hemorrhoid
- Uterus
- Asthma point
- Sciatic point
- Constipation
- Genital organs
- Urethra
- Anus
- External ear
- Rectum
- Thirst point
- Trachea
- Nose
- Hunger point
- Hypertension
- Blood pressure Raising
- Forehead
- Neurasthenia
- Anesthetic
- Tooth point
- Tongue

- Shenmen window of the sky
- Bladder
- Lumbago
- Kidneys
- Gall bladder
- Large intestine
- Liver
- Small intestine
- Stomach
- Spleen
- Thyroid gland
- Lungs
- Heart
- Lungs
- Internal ear
- Eye
- Lips

Ring the tuning fork which corresponds to the area of pain as shown in the chart.

82

Sound and the Spiral of the Ear

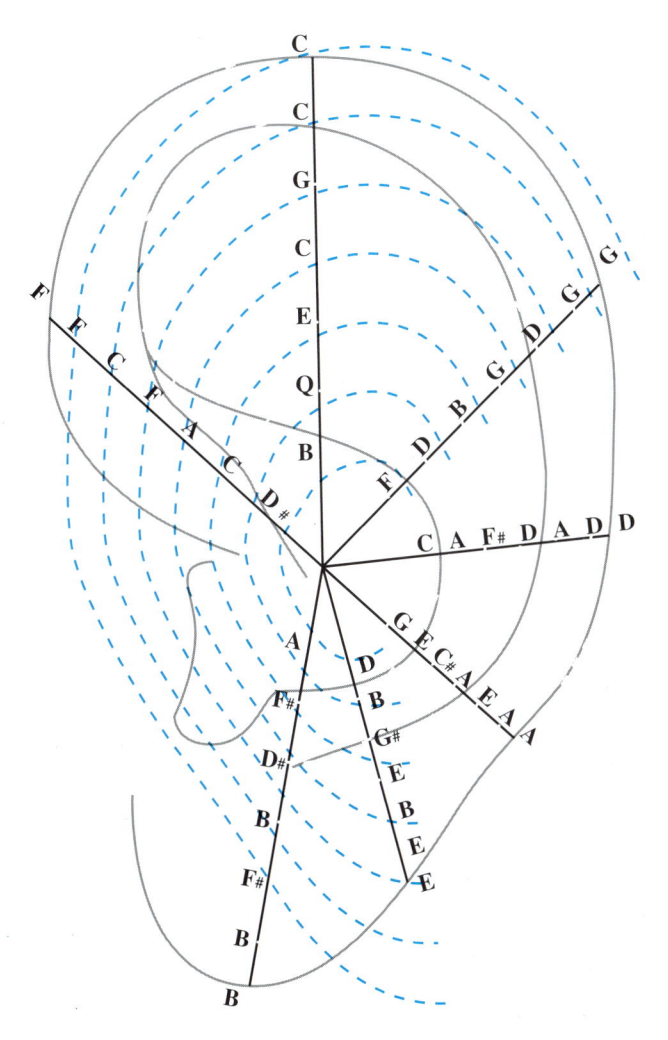

In the ear, the sound reflexology works according to zone and not organ.

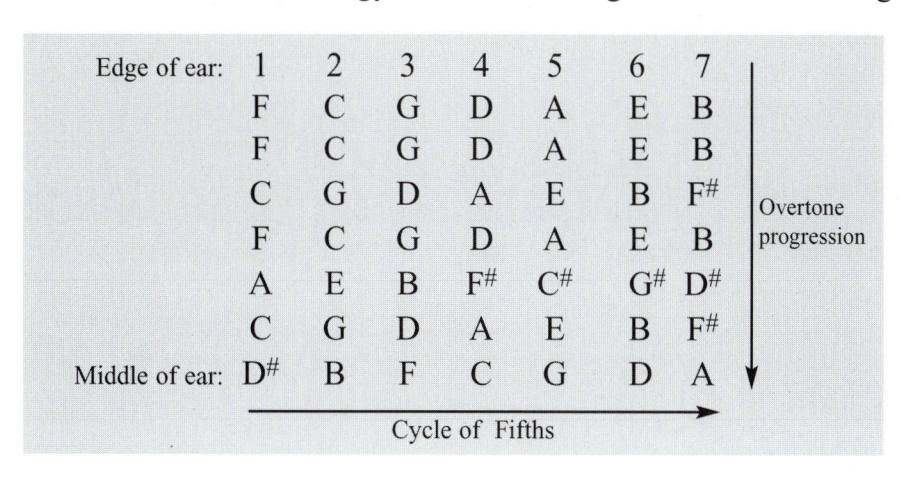

Edge of ear:	1	2	3	4	5	6	7	
	F	C	G	D	A	E	B	
	F	C	G	D	A	E	B	
	C	G	D	A	E	B	F#	Overtone
	F	C	G	D	A	E	B	progression
	A	E	B	F#	C#	G#	D#	
	C	G	D	A	E	B	F#	
Middle of ear:	D#	B	F	C	G	D	A	↓

Cycle of Fifths →

83

Musical Spine

The spine is the central axis of the physical body. The spine is linked with the chakras and the endocrine glands, with the network of the nervous system and with two important acupuncture meridians, the bladder meridian and the yang energy of Du Mai, which is the Governor meridian in the center of the spine.

One of the channels of the bladder meridian actually traces the outline of the vertebrae of the spine from the first vertebra to the sacrum. The points along the bladder meridian on both sides of the spine are known as the energetical reflex points of all the organs of the body. The spine is also the link between the ganglia inside and the chakras outside of the body. Thus the spine appears to be the link between inner and outer energy.

The essence of the spine is like solid sound and responds beautifully to sound healing. I use different fundamental notes for each part of the spine. Also, each zone of the spine corresponds with a musical mode and the different notes of this musical mode are applicable to each vertebra. Some modes will relax the spine, while other modes will stimulate the spine. We can use tuning forks, tubes, xylophone or the piano. Sound and color are used here in a different scale of reference linked with the astral level and no longer with the physical/etheric level like the sound used in acupuncture which is given in Chinese Five Element Theory.

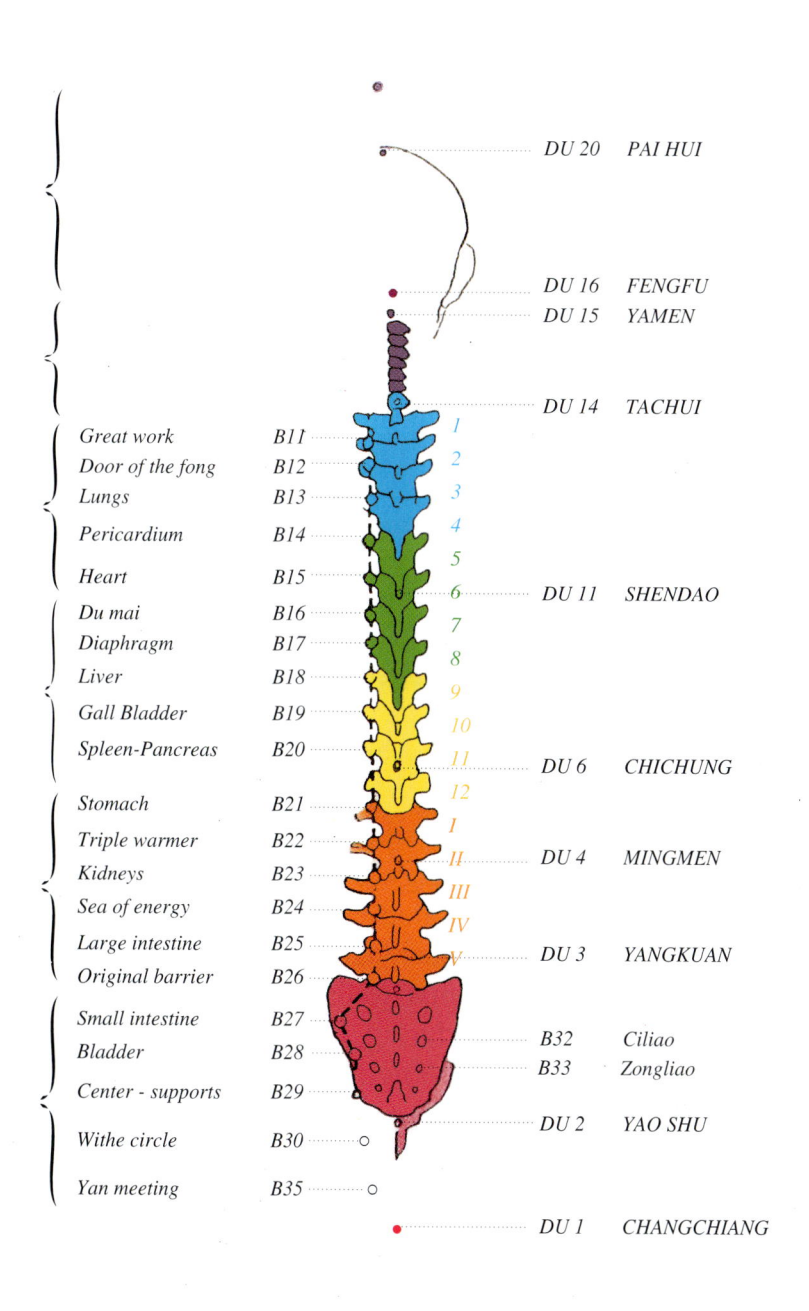

			DU 20	PAI HUI
			DU 16	FENGFU
			DU 15	YAMEN
			DU 14	TACHUI
Great work	B11	1		
Door of the fong	B12	2		
Lungs	B13	3		
Pericardium	B14	4		
Heart	B15	5		
		6	DU 11	SHENDAO
Du mai	B16	7		
Diaphragm	B17	8		
Liver	B18	9		
Gall Bladder	B19	10		
Spleen-Pancreas	B20	11	DU 6	CHICHUNG
		12		
Stomach	B21	I		
Triple warmer	B22	II	DU 4	MINGMEN
Kidneys	B23	III		
Sea of energy	B24	IV		
Large intestine	B25	V	DU 3	YANGKUAN
Original barrier	B26			
Small intestine	B27			
Bladder	B28		B32	Ciliao
Center - supports	B29		B33	Zongliao
Withe circle	B30		DU 2	YAO SHU
Yan meeting	B35			
			DU 1	CHANGCHIANG

THE MASTER POINTS OF THE SPINE

The zones of the spine correspond and vibrate differently with each season during the year. Each zone resonates with a musical mode, key and color as seen in the following chart.

The sacrum resonates with earth and Indian summer, the color red, and modes Vibhasa and Jog in the key of F.

The orange zone, the five lumbar, resonates with water and winter, and modes Hindol and Gunkali in the key of C

The yellow zone, thoracic vertebrae 12 - 9 resonates with wood and spring, and modes Bhupala and Durga in the key of G.

The green zone, thoracic vertebrae 8 - 5, resonates with fire and summer, and modes Megha and Bhupali in the key of D.

The blue zone, thoracic vertebrae 4 - 1 resonates with metal and autumn, and modes Sri and Malkaus in the key of A.

The purple zone, cervical vertebrae 7 - 1 plus the head, resonates with the overtone progression from E to B, Sky resonance.

The spine is the witness of karma and also a strong mirror of ones present life. The spine offers an understanding of physical, emotional and mental problems if you are aware of the zone which is affected. There are two important points linked with the energy of karma in the spine: Mingmen, called the "door of destiny" located between the second and third lumbar and Yangkuan on the fifth lumbar, called the "original barrier." All other points from the base of the spine to the top will develop the ability to unfold this energy of karma during each person's lifetime according with the degree of opening of Mingmen and Yangkuan. We should always send chi to these two points to open the way!

The musical progression along the spine is a gentle yet powerful tool for releasing physical tension in the spine and harmonizing the back area with the most important reflex zone in the human body. The sounds of the musical modes help to awaken memories from past, present and future lives.

		B6					B6	RESONANCE WITH SKY
		A#			TEP 9		A#	GUIDANCE BY COSMIC
		G#					G#	"CHI"
HARMONIC		F#			TEP 8		F#	HARMONIC
PROGRESSION		E					E	PROGRESSION
		D					D	
		B					B	
		G#					G#	
		E5					E5	
		B					B	
		E4					E4	
SRI		A			TEP 7		A	MALKAUS
DISPERSE		G#					G	HARMONIZE
STIMULATE		E					F	RELAX
AUTUMN		D			TEP 6		D	AUTUMN
		A#					C	
		A4		1			A4	
MEGHA		D		2			D	BHUPALI
DISPERSE		C		3			B	HARMONIZE
STIMULATE		A	Lungs	4			A	RELAX
SUMMER		G		5			F#	SUMMER
		E	Heart	6	TEP 5		E	
		D4		7			D4	
BHUPALA		G		8			G	DURGA
DISPERSE		D#	SHEN	9			E	HARMONIZE
STIMULATE		D	Liver	10			D	RELAX
SPRING		A#		11			C	SPRING
		G#	Spleen	12	TEP 13c		A	
		G3		I			G4	
HINDOL		C		II			C	GUNKALI
DISPERSE		B		III	TEP 4		G#	HARMONIZE
STIMULATE		A	Kidneys	IV			G	RELAX
WINTER		F#		V			F	WINTER
		E			TEP 3		C#	
		C3					C3	
		F					F	
VIBHASA		D					Eb	JOG
DISPERSE		C					C	HARMONIZE
STIMULATE		B			TEP 2		Bb	RELAX
INTER-SEASON		A					A	INTER-SEASON
							G#	
		F#					F2	ANCHOR
		F2						TO CENTER
								OF AXIS
		D2	KNEE		Knee		D2	RESONANCE
								WITH EARTH
FUNDAMENTAL		A#1	HEEL		TEP 1		A#1	GUIDANCE
								BY EARTH "CHI"

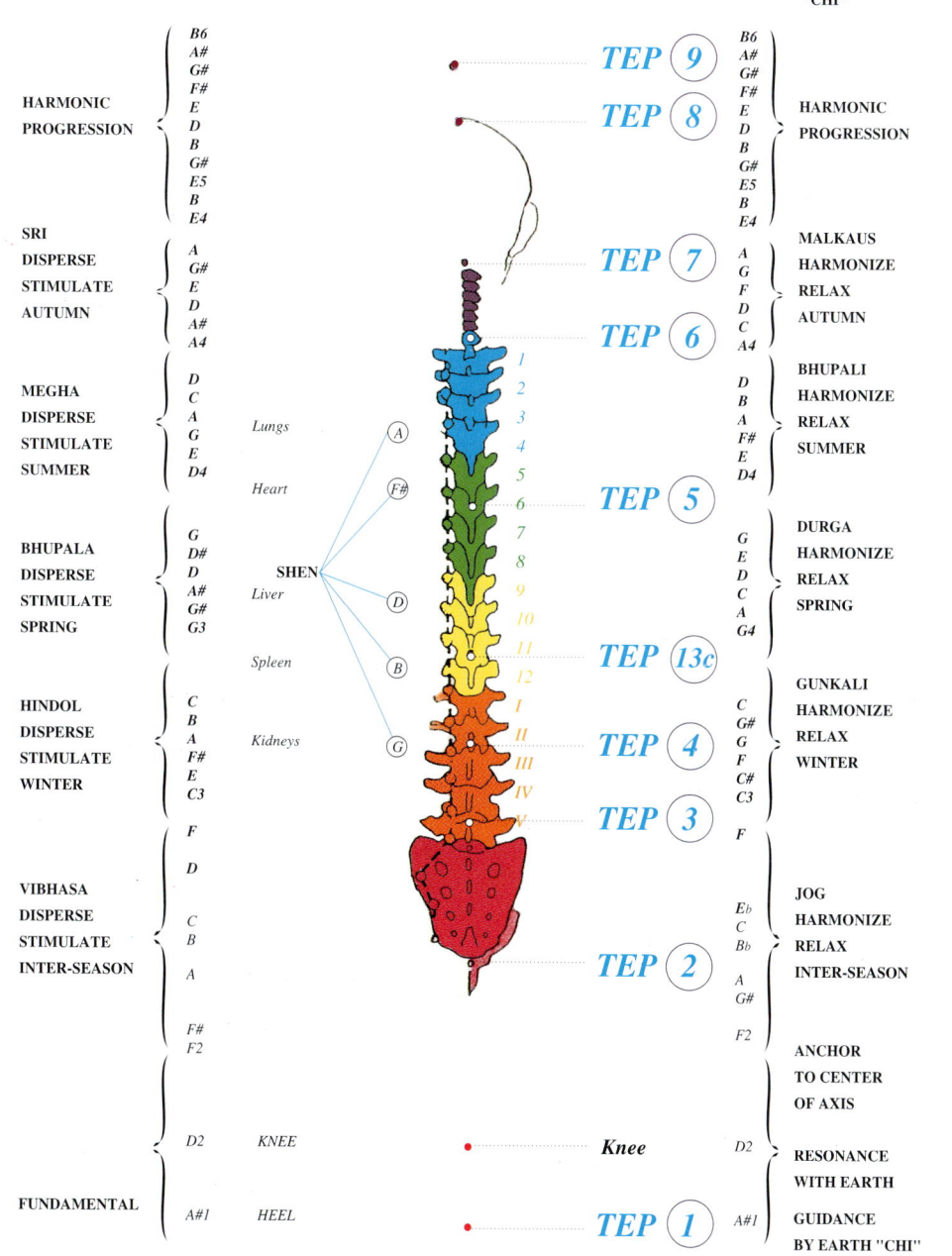

THE SPINE VIBRATES DIFFERENTLY WITH EACH SEASON
EACH SEASON RESONATES WITH A MUSICAL MODE
THROUGH THE CHOICE OF MODE, WE CAN EITHER HARMONIZE OR STIMULATE

THE MUSICAL SPINE

Sound and Acupuncture

In sound healing there are different scales of correspondence depending on whether one is working on the physical level, astral level or mental level. The key of each season given by the Chinese works on the physical level according with the Law of the Five Elements. The first spine chart, The Master Points of the Spine, shows how to work on the spine from the astral level with sounding tubes. The scale outside of the physical body in the astral level, from the sacrum to the cervical, follows the Cycle of Fifths progression.

In the second spine chart the musical modes are shown in two columns, one to the left of the spine and one to the right of the spine. On the left are all of the modes used to stimulate the different zones. On the right are all of the releasing and harmonizing modes. You will play for each zone the appropriate mode either with the sounding tubes, with the piano or with a monochord table about 30 centimeters from the spine. You can also play all of the modes from the sacrum to the cervical, one by one very slowly in the appropriate rhythm to harmonize or stimulate the spine.[14]

Stimulating   *Modes*
Vibhasa: Key of F
Hindol: Key of C
Bhupala: Key of G
Megha: Key of D
Sri: Key of A
Harmonic progression from E to B

Relaxing   *Modes*
Jog: Key of F
Gunkali: Key of C
Durga: Key of G
Bhupali: Key of D
Malkaus: Key of A
Harmonic progression from E to B

Chapter Five

Esoteric Resonance: Sound, Acupuncture and Kototama

Kototama, Science of Pure Sound

The World, the Logos, or Tao, is composed of fifty sounds, each uniquely contributing to the creation of the universe. With full human development, our actual capacity becomes one with creative power. This is the inheritance of our human spirit. Today each one of us is recognizing and realizing the world according to our own individual and separate capacity. There is a natural order in the world around us and within us, but we have forgotten how to follow this order. Thus we... are suffering in our society and we have no hope of a better tomorrow.

The sound principles teach us how to put our physical lives in perfect order with the universe. The spoken word (and world), fully synchronized with the outside and the inside will close the gap between spirit and matter.

Sensei Nakazono, 1972

Kototama is an ancient science of pure sound. Though the original roots of Kototama are unknown, this esoteric teaching has been transmitted secretly and orally within the Japanese culture for the last 2000 years. When Sensei Nakazono, my Master of Aikido, acupuncture and Kototama, first began teaching Kototama outside of Japan in 1972, there was a synchronistic worldwide awakening to the mysteries and powers of sound.

Sound and Acupuncture

The sound structure of consciousness which Kototama describes can be integrated into the Chinese Five Element Theory to create a strong lens through which to view the human being in resonance with nature. Kototama sound can bring information to the body through the five elements and can also be used to stimulate the physical organs and the acupuncture meridians.

The Kototama vowel sounds are used to stimulate the Yin organs. A consonant with the vowel stimulates the Yang organs. As you sing the sound from the chart below visualize the corresponding color and place your hands over the area where the organ is located in the body. You may feel your hands being moved gently into the auric space of the organ. If so, sound more quietly or move into overtoning until you end with your hands far into the aura of the organ, just thinking the sound.

Element	Organ	Note	Color	Sound
Earth	Stomach	A	Yellow	WI
	Spleen-Pancreas	A#		I
First Fire	Heart	B	Red	E
	Small Intestine	C		WE
Water	Bladder	C#	Dark blue	WO
	Kidney	D		O
Second Fire	Pericardium	D#	Crimson	HI
	Triple Warmer	E		HWI
Wood	Gall Bladder	F	Green	WA
	Liver	F#		A
Metal	Large Intestine	G	White	U
	Lungs	G#		WU

Kototama sounds are not pronounced like the English vowels are pronouced. In Kototama: I = $\bar{\text{E}}$, E = $\bar{\text{A}}$, A = AH, O is the same as in English, and U is OO (as on boot).

The visualization of the color added to the resonance of your own voice singing these sounds will do much to stimulate your internal energy system.[15]

Sound Structures: Space and Time

Kototama practices could be called meditations of sound which contain cosmic memories of the sound structure of the universe as well as vibrational influences of civilizations past, present and future. At the same time, this sound science reaches the deep level of the internal organs of the physical body through a resonance with the five elements and acupuncture.

In an attempt to provide a philosophical overview of the creation of the world using the semantics of sound, Kototama works with the energetic meanings of the vowels and consonants. These linguistic sound units form the roots of all languages and also provide a sound structure for understanding the creative manifestation of the universe.

Vowels carry magnetic power and thus create the spatial dimension of sound as it continues to spiral through space - beginning with the Original Sound (the Big Bang, The Word, the Logos, or "U" in Kototama). With their electric power, the pure consonant sounds introduce the more human concept of time. So, while vowels open space, consonants mark time. Vowels and consonants, arranged in different orders or sequences in Kototama, define specific epochs in human evolution. These orders of sound are introduced in Book IV of this series.

The practice of Kototama vowels and consonant orders which are presented in Book IV can help to awaken us to our inherent multidimensionality. When the pure sounds of Kototama can be linked with our physical structure through the internal organs, this multidimensionality can be integrated into the body. It is through the principles of acupuncture and the Law of the Five Elements that the Kototama sounds finds resonance with the physical body.

Kototama Sounds and Acupuncture with Musical Notes

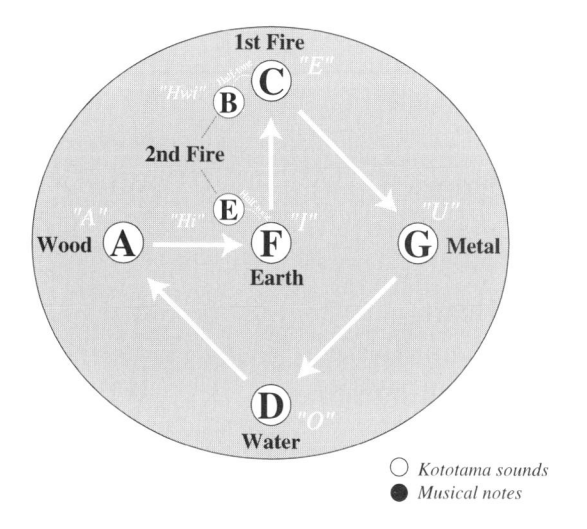

Musical Notes for the Six Elements with the Six Sounds which Stimulate the Six Noble Organs.

The earth is the center and begins the cycle in the "Little Circulation" which proceeds in this order: Earth, First Fire, Metal, Water, Wood, Second Fire. In this order, you also realize the Cycle of the Fifths, F C G D A E B

In the Ionian Scale (of the Pythagorean or Greek Modes) there are two half tones: E to F and B to C. These two intervals have an energetic meaning and special function.[16]

    E = Pericardium, the higher state of earth: The fire energy of birth returns to the earth element as the energy of incarnation. E "returns" to F, realizing the half tone interval.

    B = Triple Warmer and is the higher state of the First Fire (Heart). The fire of the soul energy "returns" to the fire of the heart as the energy of transmutation. B returns to C.

Sound and Acupuncture

Correspondence: Element - Organ - Sound - Note in the "Little Circulation" when using the Human Voice for Harmonization

Element	Organ	Sound	Note
EARTH	Spleen	I	F
	Stomach	WI	
FIRST FIRE	Heart	E	C
	Small Intestine	WE	
METAL	Lungs	U	G
	Large Intestine	WU	
WATER	Kidneys	O	D
	Bladder	WO	
WOOD	Liver	A	A
	Gall Bladder	WA	
SECOND FIRE	Pericardium	HI	E / B
	Triple Heater	HWI	

Remember: In Kototama sound the vowel pronunciation is different from the English pronunciation: A is pronounced AH, E is pronounced $\overline{A}$, I is pronounced $\overline{E}$, O is pronounced $\overline{O}$ and U is pronounced OO.

The Second Fire has two different musical notes for Yin and Yang because of its energetic particularity: The Second Fire originates the two half tones of the scale and the two fundamental functions in life, incarnation and transmutation.

Generally Kototama Sounds are only used to stimulate Yin organs with one pitch for each element, just as the Chinese Breath (shown in Book IV) which sedates Yin organs also uses one pitch for each element.

When we use the voice for sounding in Kototama we follow the Law of the Five Elements, (the "Little Circulation") and use the musical note for each organ which is given in the Law of the Five Elements.

When we use musical instruments and tuning forks for sounding, we follow the progression of the "Big Circulation," the Chinese Twenty-Four Hour Energetic clock. Here the musical correspondence is not the same as it is when the voice is used for sounding. This is because the inner resonance of the sound of one's own voice is not the same as the outer resonance which comes from an instrument.

In the "Little Circulation," the earth, note F, is the center and as such is the master point on which the musical progression is built. In the "Big Circulation," the wood, specifically the gall bladder, is the master point. The gall bladder becomes the "decision maker" around which all other organs are placed. The F of earth in the "Little Circulation" becomes the A of wood in the "Big Circulation."

The stomach, which is normally earth and F, becomes A in the Chinese Twenty-Four Hour Energetic Clock and the liver and the gall bladder become F and F# respectively. This inversion between wood and earth reflects the spiritual relationship between wood and earth: earth gives space and place to the wood. When the wood dies, it returns as nourishment into earth. A circle of life is established. Also, when the tree receives light from the sun, this light is felt by the earth as a transformative force.

Sound and Acupuncture

The Song of the Triple Warmer

The Kototama Sounds and the musical notes for each organ combine to create an interesting healing song which I call "The Song of the Triple Warmer." If you have read the sections on Brazilian music in Book I of this series, *The Role of Music in the Twenty-First Century*, you will not be too amazed to find that the melody of the Triple Warmer song is exactly the same melody which is found in a Brazilian song called "Indiu." This song, which was composed by Joao Gilberto, creator of the Bossa Nova, is also sung using pure sound - no words.

The Song of the Triple Warmer with the sound of Kototama

Musical Notes and Harmony by Fabien Maman

Musical Notes and Sounds of the Triple Warmer

C WE (Small Intestine)	*G* U (Lungs)	*C* WE (Small Intestine)	*E* I (Spleen)
C WE (Small Intestine)	*G* U (Lungs)	*C* WE (Small Intestine)	*E* I (Spleen)
C WE (Small Intestine)	*G* U (Lungs)	*C* WE (Small Intestine)	*E* I (Spleen)
C WE (Small Intestine)	*E* HWI (Triple Warmer)		
C WE (Small Intestine)	*E* HWI (Triple Warmer)	*C* WE (Small Intestine)	*D* O (Kidney)
C WE (Small Intestine)	*E* HWI (Triple Warmer)	*C* WE (Small Intestine)	*D* O (Kidney)
C WE (Small Intestine)	*E* HWI (Triple Warmer)	*C* WE (Small Intestine)	*D* O (Kidney)
A A (Liver)	*C* WE (Small Intestine)		

Chapter Six

The Chart of the Eight Elements

The Chart of the Eight Elements is a tool which places the human being at birth in resonance with the greater energy patterns of sky and earth that will influence lifelong physical, psychological and spiritual temperament. I think of this tool as a continuation of the relationship between sound and acupuncture in which earth and cosmos, matter and spirit, body and sound are combined into a specific structure consisting of eight elements as shown below.

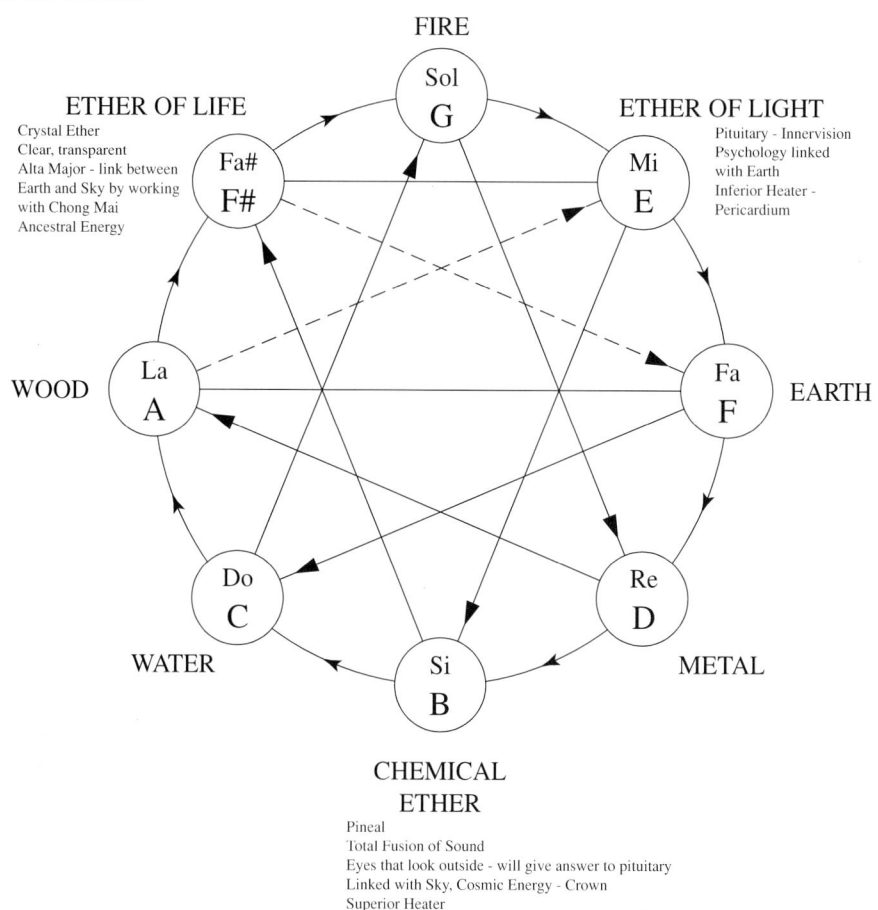

FIRE — Sol / G

ETHER OF LIFE — Fa# / F#
Crystal Ether
Clear, transparent
Alta Major - link between Earth and Sky by working with Chong Mai
Ancestral Energy

ETHER OF LIGHT — Mi / E
Pituitary - Innervision
Psychology linked with Earth
Inferior Heater - Pericardium

WOOD — La / A

EARTH — Fa / F

WATER — Do / C

METAL — Re / D

CHEMICAL ETHER — Si / B
Pineal
Total Fusion of Sound
Eyes that look outside - will give answer to pituitary
Linked with Sky, Cosmic Energy - Crown
Superior Heater

I developed this Chart of the Eight Elements in order to work with the cosmic energies directly in the body, in the meridians. The Eight Element Chart explains the full scope of our existence here on earth, whereas the five elements only explain the physical dimension. The connection with the eight elements carries the meaning of life itself in its totality by creating a form in which to understand the relationship between the elemental essences of life. In other words, the infusion of the three ethers, which represent the soul, with the five elements brings forth a new relationship with nature, each other and the universe that can be integrated at the physical level.

The Meaning of the Three Ethers

The ETHER OF LIGHT corresponds to the pituitary gland, the third eye, inner vision, introspection, and the link with the Ajna chakra. The pituitary gland is connected with the psychological and emotional understanding of life. It is the Light in each of us, connected with the notion of space. This center is also called the Inferior Ether, according to Rudolph Steiner, because it is linked by the pericardium to sexual energy.

The CHEMICAL ETHER corresponds to the pineal gland which integrates the total fusion of the vibration of sound. The pineal gland is the symbolic fourth eye, the eye that looks outward, the answer to the third eye. Linked with the Sahasara chakra, this center is the one that can answer, in time, to the message or information coming from the pituitary gland through the hypothalamus. This ether is linked with the sky and with cosmic knowledge. It is also called the Superior Ether by Rudolph Steiner.

The ETHER OF LIFE is called the divine or crystal ether because every level of life becomes clear and transparent when this dimension is penetrated. There is no need to explain anything. You are life itself in full consciousness. This ether is linked with the crystal light which is sitting in Alta Major, the Occipital chakra or seat of unlimited consciousness.

When you integrate your inner vision with cosmic knowledge, the channel meridian, Chong Mai, becomes open for you to make the link between earth and sky. Your ancestral memories will return and the synthesis will be made in the heart, as it is for the Five Shen.

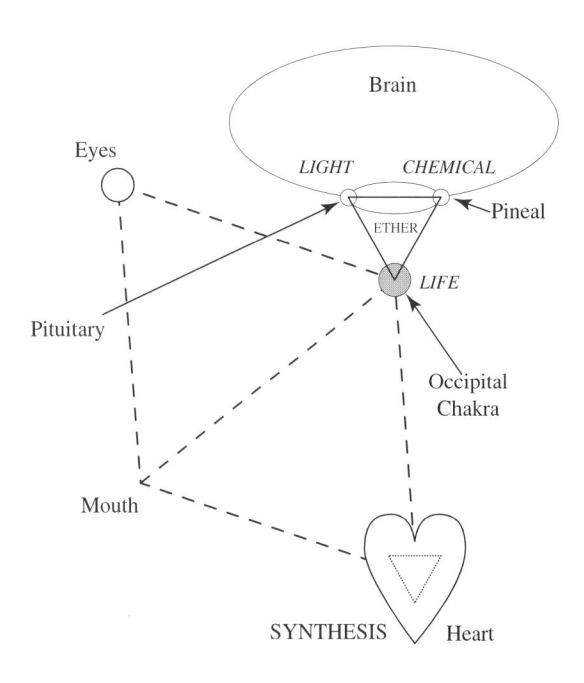

You will notice that I have included the musical notes on the Chart of the Eight Elements (page 99) in a Cycle of Fifths beginning with the earth element. Musically, the chart will stabilize as follows:

Chart of the 8 Elements

F - EARTH
C - WATER
G - FIRE
D - AIR, METAL
A - WOOD
E - ETHER OF LIGHT
B - CHEMICAL ETHER
F# - ETHER OF LIFE (here change level, octave)

Chart of the 5 Elements

F - EARTH
C - FIRE
G - AIR, METAL
D - WATER
A - WOOD

This musical progression follows the complete Cycle of Fifths, which stimulates the expansion of life on all levels of development. The musical meaning of the interval between the two charts (the musical change between the eight element chart and the five element chart) will shed some new light on the understanding of the integration of the elements.

Here, as in the following chart, we see that precise musical law has been adhered to in the Theory of the Eight Elements. The notes fall "right" and empower the existing Law of the Five Elements. Anytime a mathematical law agrees with theory, it verifies the truth of the theory. We see, then, that the progression of the musical notes proves the structure of the elements.

Analogy of the Musical Structures Corresponding to the Elements
Terrestrial and Cosmic Energy

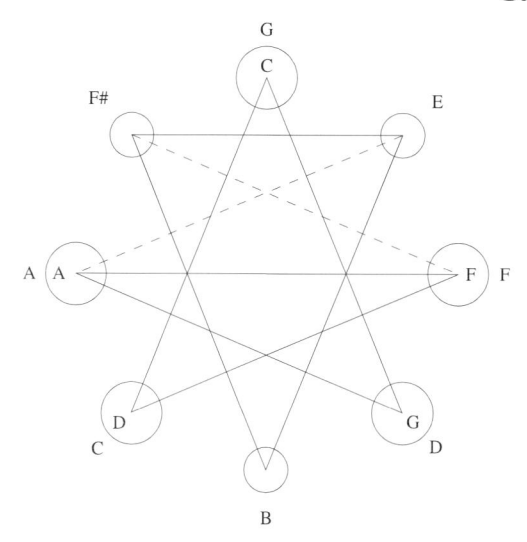

The astral plane - connection to terrestrial energy (5 Elements)
The mental plane - connection to cosmic energy   (8 Elements)

Musical Intervals between the Five Elements and the Eight Elements

F	Interval	Octave	Opening of the 3 Ethers Terrestrial Energy
C	Interval	Second	Opposes Water and Fire
G	Interval	Fifth	Amplifies Fire and Air
D	Interval	Fourth	Tension of Metal and Wood
A	Interval	Octave	Opening of the 3 Ethers Celestial Energy
E	Interval	Fifth	Ether of Light
B	Interval	Fifth	Chemical Ether
F#	Interval	Fifth	Ether of Life Wood of the Tree of Life Spiral towards the Sky Maximum Interval before next level (octave) Finishing the octave Woods returns to Earth

The energetic relationship among the eight elements follows the model of the integration of life since conception as explained on page 111:

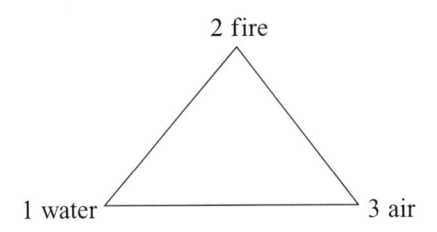

```
           2 fire
           /\
          /  \
         /    \
        /_____\
   1 water    3 air
```

In this model of integration, air is associated with metal as in acupuncture. Also, water includes wood. Wood depends upon water and does not appear as a basic element like water, fire, and air.

So for the stimulation of the triangle of the three ethers,

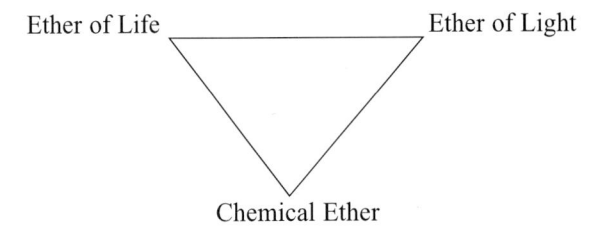

```
Ether of Life _____ Ether of Light
              \      /
               \    /
                \  /
                 \/
           Chemical Ether
```

we use the first triangle of fire, air/metal, and water/wood.

The stimulation of the Ether of Light is accomplished by the fire of the pericardium. The stimulation of the Chemical Ether is completed by the air (prana) of the lungs. The stimulation of the Ether of Life is realized through the liver (center of the Mystical Axis which is described in the Appendix). Here the wood of the liver is carried through the element water. The kidneys represent the Light of Life. The kidneys are at the base of the pyramid of vital energy: Yuan Chi.

The mother, water, is expressed here by her son, the wood. The stimulation is accomplished by using the three notes, G, D, A as a chord of resonance. Water and wood here are like the flower and the fruit. They come from Light. Light produces life in the physical body through the integration and absorption of the fruit.

In the Law of the Eight Elements, the inhibition is accomplished by the Three Ethers among themselves. Inhibition does not occur separately. The resonance of the three notes E, B and F# played successively work to rebalance in the Law of the Eight Elements. The sounds used are produced by long tubes of resonance with low frequencies which produce high overtones. The sound of these tubes allows the energetic link with the Three Ethers which are the doors of the soul. The following chapter continues the explanation of the Three Ethers.

The Law of the Eight Elements works uniquely on the Three Ethers incorporated with the Five Elements in order to facilitate the evolution of human consciousness.

Both through acupuncture and music, this Chart of the Eight Elements offers the possibility of incorporating the soul into everyday life. It offers a concrete tool which fine tunes the ability to diagnose imbalance from a more psychological point of view and beyond.

This chart also changes the way we view life and love. What will it mean to us, for example, that now we can understand the higher cause of many people's liver problems today? This chart reveals that the liver/wood is the energetic key to all spiritual questions because it is the center of the Mystical Axis (see Appendix).

Soon we will understand that a small gesture, such as repressing another person's inner vision, will create a blockage in the energy of the liver of this person. This chart also reveals that each of us work in the same patterns of physicality, regardless of gender. In the end, all our earth elements are the same - skeletons lying in the sun. And all of our ethers come from the same source of light. With this chart we also shed some light on the period between two lifetimes. An advantage is that the Law of the Eight Elements works almost like the Five Element Chart in acupuncture except the little subtlety added to move the energy in the Three Ethers.

Chapter Seven

Prenatal Alchemical Etheric Cycle

The Prenatal Alchemical Etheric Cycle is, in its simplest form, a chart of divination which I developed in order to expand the current forms of astrological divination, both eastern and western. This chart is designed to address the emotional, physical, spiritual and cosmic significance of birthtime, in addition to providing specific avenues through which to heal the body and enlighten the soul's journey through this particular lifetime.

Using this cycle is not about inserting numbers into a formula and translating astrological angles into concepts. It is about understanding a new way of life. Through this subtle process we begin to understand the roots of our temperament and typology - the roots of our deep being - in psychological and emotional terms. We also learn which spiritual way will be ours and how our personal karma will use one of the elements to express itself if needed.

The Prenatal Alchemical Etheric Cycle is composed of three parts:
   1. Synchronization
   2. Integration
   3. Transformation

Synchronization concerns the process of incarnation itself. The moment of birth is crucial in determining how the energy runs in our meridians for the rest of our lives. Depending on the hour of birth, we receive energy through whatever organ is strongest during that time according to the twenty-four hour clock in acupuncture.

Depending on the season, we also receive energy through the organs that are ruled by the element of this season. According to the chart on page 110, a child born at 7:00 p.m. in July would receive energy first through the area of her pericardium (corresponding to the hour of birth). If the birth happened relatively easily, this child will have strong pericardium energy. If the birth was difficult, long or traumatic, it would be necessary to locate the time of the trauma during labor and use this time as the point at which the energy was first translated. Therefore, a child born under hard conditions would be born with weak organs corresponding to the time of trauma. The chart is shown in a fixed position, but the wheels rotate to accommodate any birth situation.

Newborn babies synchronize with the world through sound. They cannot speak or cannot "feel" themselves as individual, but they can "hear" through vibration. Newborns take in the energy of sound through vibration. When they are held, they "feel" their mother's blood pumping or the sound her bones make when she walks. Babies hear with their newly developing cells, not with their ears, and all sound from the "outside," however far out in the cosmos, is translated for them through the sound of one of the five elements.

When we are born, we experience the vibration of sound in two fundamental forms: the Cycle of Fifths and the progression of overtones. Vibration that comes to us along the body or up and down the spine or through the chakras, for example, follows the Cycle of Fifths. Sound that enters the body deeply, to the cells of the organs, follows the progression of overtones as it travels inward and this we respond to later in life.

Notice how the following chart has the ear substituted for the fetus in the second diagram. What we do with the ear as children and adults we do with our whole body at the moment of birth. Newborns are constantly translating sound in their bodies. If a normal pattern of sound is disrupted at birth then the normal pattern of energy translation will also be disrupted and the organs will be adversely affected, just as if the labor had been overly hard.

For example, children who were born during World War II when bomb sirens were constantly sounding, experienced a severe distortion in the soundfields around them. As a result, the sound vibration that was to be received in the meridians was disturbed, causing an organ weakness or an unusual reflex to develop.

I know a person who was born under such wartime conditions and each time he feels stress he responds by overeating. He was born in the morning between seven and nine o'clock when the energy is in the stomach. The sound of the sirens and the fear of his mother went directly into his stomach and this sound pattern still resides there, so that his stomach is activated each time he becomes fearful or agitated.

The following chart shows synchronization between the Chinese Twenty-Four Hour Enegy Clock and the western and eastern correspondence of astrological elements with the organs.

SYNCHRONIZATION

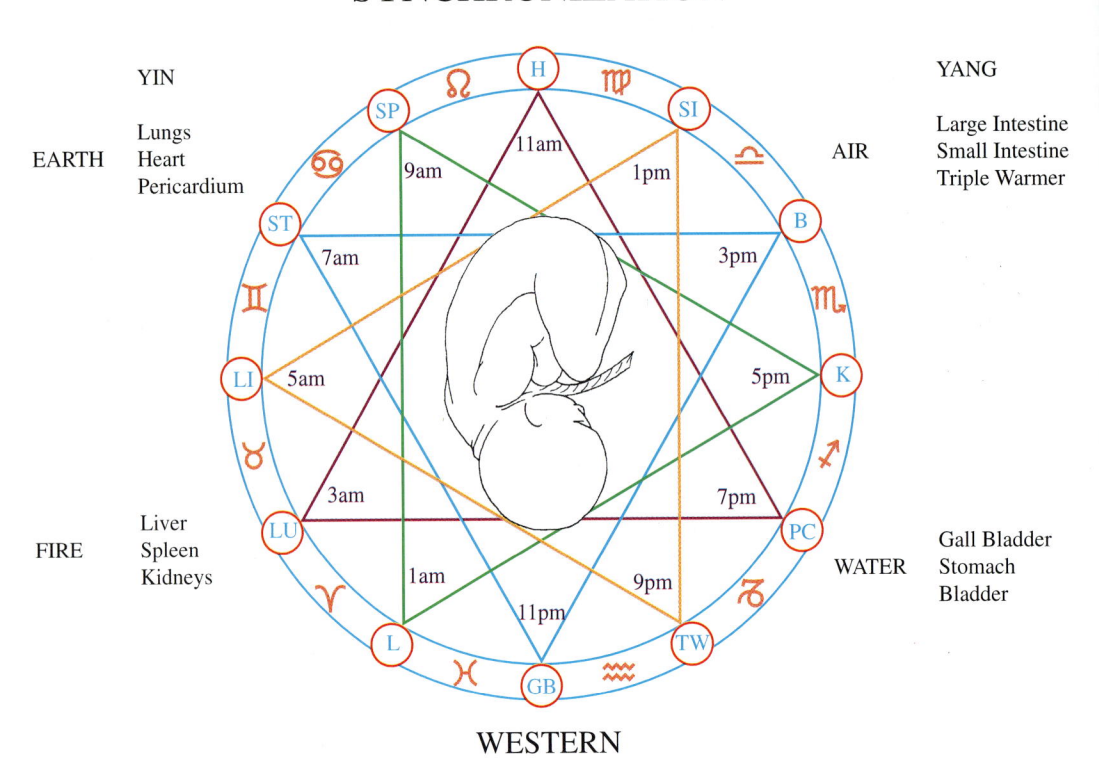

WESTERN

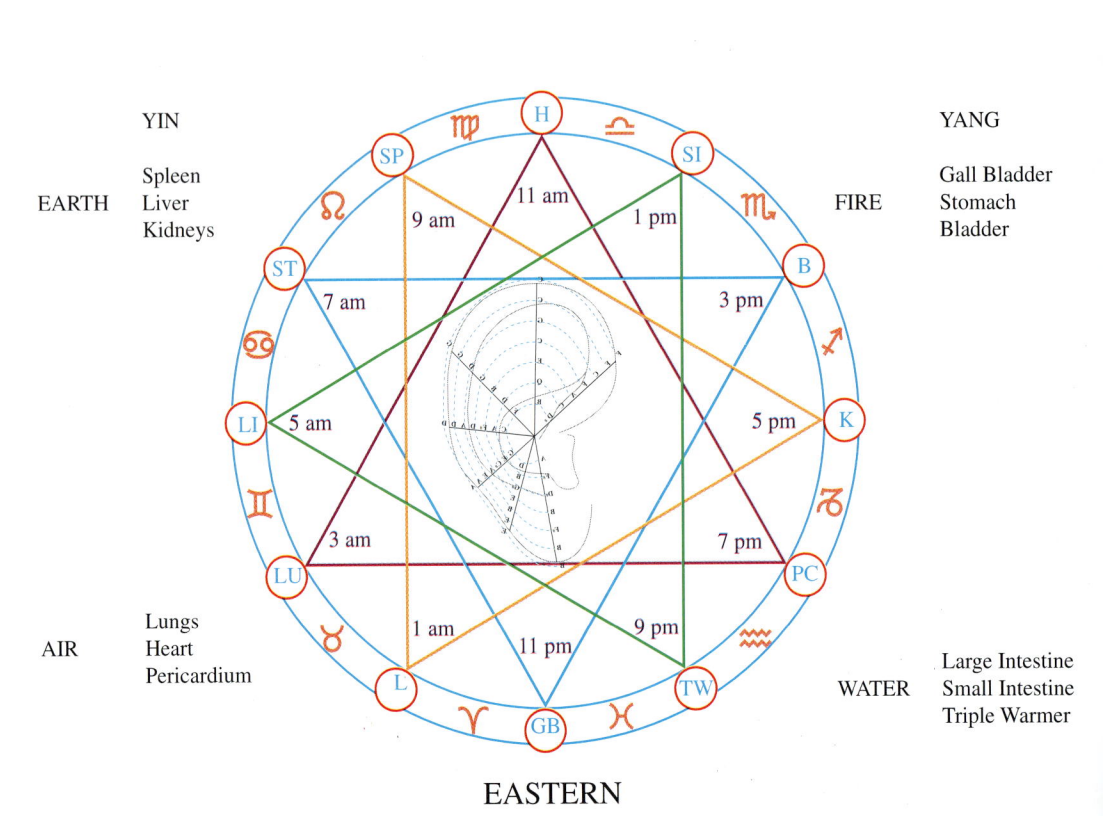

YIN
EARTH — Lungs, Heart, Pericardium
FIRE — Liver, Spleen, Kidneys

YANG
AIR — Large Intestine, Small Intestine, Triple Warmer
WATER — Gall Bladder, Stomach, Bladder

Times: 11am (H/SP), 1pm (SI), 3pm (B), 5pm (K), 7pm (PC), 9pm (TW), 11pm (GB), 1am (L), 3am (LU), 5am (LI), 7am (ST), 9am (SP)

EASTERN

YIN
EARTH — Spleen, Liver, Kidneys
AIR — Lungs, Heart, Pericardium

YANG
FIRE — Gall Bladder, Stomach, Bladder
WATER — Large Intestine, Small Intestine, Triple Warmer

110

SYNCHRONIZATION

The preceding chart is intended to make more clear some of the ways in which sound and the moment of birth affect us. The only difference between the two diagrams, apart from the ear and the fetus, is that the top diagram is based upon western astrology and the bottom is based upon eastern astrology, creating a shift in the organ correspondence for each season or element. This chart elucidates the larger theory behind the process of incarnation found in this first step of synchronization.

Synchronization governs two movements in the process of incarnation - physical development and soul development.

Physical Development
The physical development of newborns
follows this elemental pattern:

Water - the time in the womb, the amniotic fluid. Here the fetus is linked with the hara (tantien) or second chakra by the umbilical cord.

Air - the moment of birth, first contact with air by the lungs.

Fire - the first time the newborn's heart beats in the air element, just after the first breath.

Notice that this pattern follows the clockwise direction of the Law of the Five Elements and, in itself, concerns earth energy, physical manifestation.

Soul Development
Integration of the Soul According to Rudolph Steiner

The second part of Synchronization involves a pattern that moves in the reverse of the first. This pattern involves the integration of the soul. The soul gradually enters the physical body over the long evolution of human history. This involves a progressive integration of the soul into the body through the physical organs which correspond to the fire, air, water and earth elements.

In evolution, this process began when the soul energy that was floating above prehistoric humans descended into the heart of the human being and touched the fire element. The fire element awakened the fire aspect, the divine aspect of the human being and for the first time in history, a spiritual consciousness was born. The awakening of the fire aspect corresponded to the time in prehistory when physical fire and its uses for warmth and cooking and light was discovered.

The fire element also initiated a new emotional level into human life. Our ancestors began their link with the divine through their belief in fire. Imagine many people huddled in a cave, each in his own corner, trying to keep warm. Suddenly someone comes in and builds a fire. Everyone soon gathers around the fire, first to get warm, but after a while the relationships among them begin changing, opening, warming, around their common fire.

This happens even today. When a person of a fire temperament arrives in a room with colder, more silent temperaments, his or her presence serves as a warming agent and the energy is unified and enlivened. The room crackles with energy because the fire touches the heart and the heart opens to the divine. It is actually the divine aspect which creates the possibility for connections between people.

As evolution continued the soul moved more deeply into the human body, reaching the air element of the body. Here the lungs were touched, creating another complete shift in human understanding. When the breath was understood and controlled, the beginning of speech was initiated. Human beings began to make sound and to learn to puncture the sound with words.

As evolution progresses the soul will incarnate the water element of the body and we will be able to control all of the liquid of the body which includes the blood, the lymph, the liquid of the brain, spine, andorgans, and the fluid of the memory.

At our point now, we are still learning to control the air element by working with the breath. Since the introduction of Yoga, Tai Chi, Tao Yin Fa, Chi Gong and Martial Arts, consciousness has been introduced into the breathing, but as a whole humanity is still in the process of "social breathing."

Social breathing belongs to a general emotional and collective reaction which belongs to the human wave. At this level, people are slaves of habit and automatic social reactions. When we start breathing consciously, we become free from the social collective. New messages are received and the way of life becomes linked with the individual's true path, rather than the social collective wave.

The last step of integration of the soul will happen when the soul energy reaches the earth element in the body. In order to spiritualize completely the matter, at this last step, the integration will reach the solid states, such as the bones and even the solid states of the cells. The spleen, stomach, and pancreas will be the organs linking with the soul in the future.

In the future if you were to cut off a finger, you would be able to reproduce it again by controlling the solid element in your body. Some human beings are able to control the fluids of the body, but very few have touched the level of the solids. Only a handful of Initiates or yogis have begun to integrate this power. Since the level of integration of the soul is linked with the spiritual path of the human being, when the soul reaches the earth element, the entire physical body will be spiritualized.

The process of integration of the soul is illustrated in the chart of synchronization as the following:

Fire - The time of the Lemurians when the cosmic fire of the sun was brought down into the human heart, when humans had internal feeling for the first time.

This process moves in a clockwise direction - like the body clock of acupuncture. It concerns earth energy.

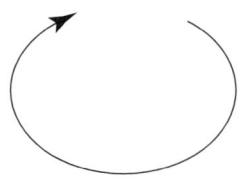

Air - The time of Atlantis when the breath first left the lungs in the form of sounds, and, later, language.

Water - The future when the water of the body will be controlled by human thought. This will be a time when humans will be able to do such things as consciously move their lymph or remove a virus from their bloodstream.

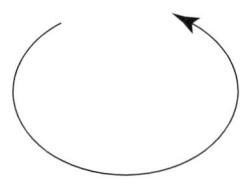

This process follows a counter-clockwise movement like the astrological wheel and, thus, is concerned with cosmic energy. The energy of physical development and the energy of the integration of the soul reflect the rotation of yin and yang and correspond to the two wheels of each chakra, which also rotate in reverse of each other. At its most fundamental level, this pattern of rotation reflects the center of the two energies - earth and sky.

This first step in the process of incarnation shown in the Prenatal Alchemical Etheric Cycle, synchronization, shows us the roots of the paradox of life based on the principle of duality: plus and minus, yin and yang, clockwise and counter-clockwise, male and female. This phenomenon must be understood from gestation to birth.

Inversion among the Elements

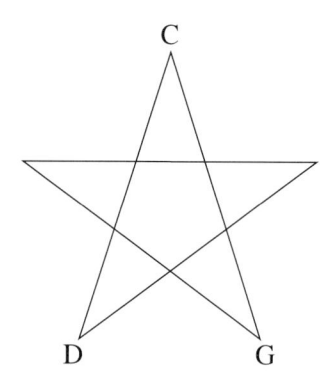

G	for air, metal	**Physical**
D	for water	
C	for fire	

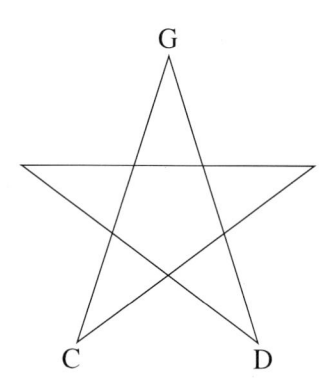

G	for fire	**Spiritual**
D	for air, metal	
C	for water	

Integration

The second process of incarnation is called integration. Here the soul, manifested by the Three Ethers of life, enters the process. The ethers breathe the spiritual and cosmic energies into our bodies. Therefore, the ethers must be incorporated into the Law of the Five Elements in order for us to understand how the spiritual affects the physical. These three ethers balance on the spiritual plane the three corresponding elements on the physical plane. This integration is the basis of the Law of the Eight Elements which is shown from a geometrical point of view in the following chart:

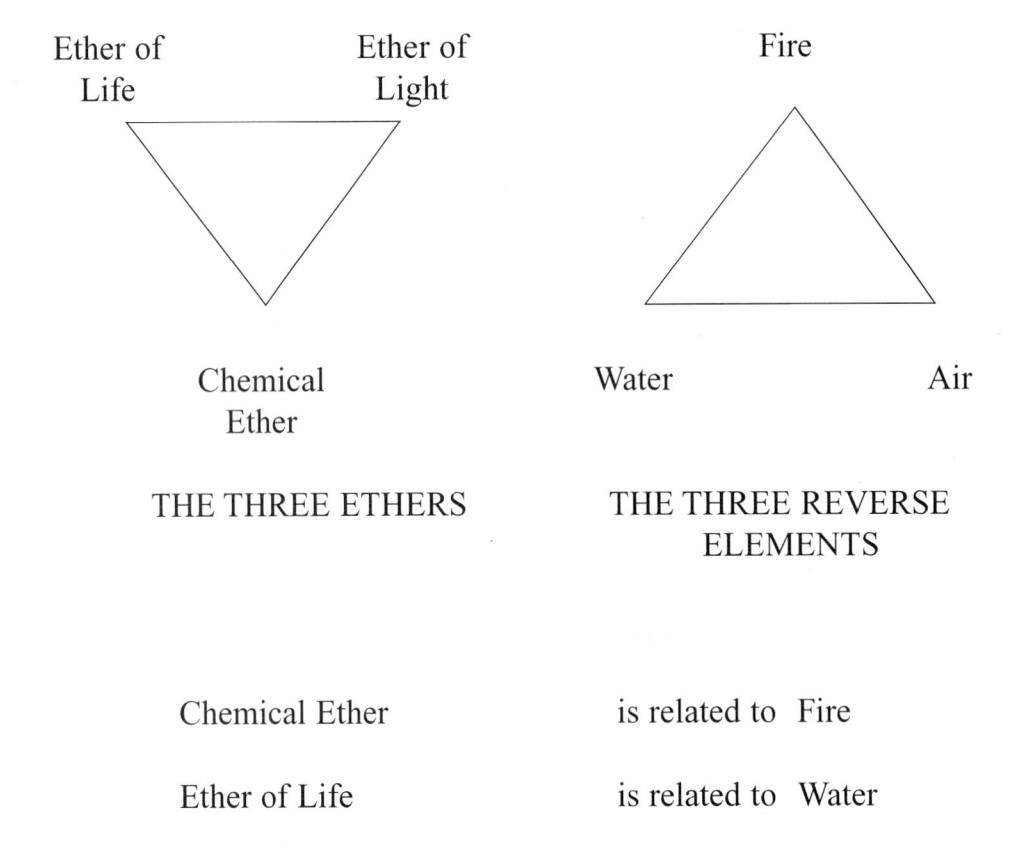

```
Ether of          Ether of                    Fire
 Life              Light
       ▽                                       △

      Chemical                  Water                    Air
       Ether

    THE THREE ETHERS              THE THREE REVERSE
                                      ELEMENTS
```

Chemical Ether   is related to Fire

Ether of Life   is related to Water

Ether of Light   is related to Air

Transformation

The final step in the process of incarnation works with ancestral energy. *This energy comes to each of us and will reach us in our lifetime.* There are eight dates in the zodiac where strong cosmic energy manifests itself. The energy that belongs to you is in accordance with the date that is closest to your birthdate.

Certain acupuncture points have a connection with this energy and time of year. They are the eight command points of the eight extra meridians. At certain times of the year you may feel unusually powerful and connected with the sky and earth, even if you do not consciously know why. Often those times correspond to one of the eight dates when cosmic energy manifests the strongest during the year. When you begin to tune with the date that corresponds to your birthday, you will be able to connect consciously with your cosmic energy and take advantage of this time by working with your energy. The acupuncture point that is the command point for your time will help you link with and integrate this cosmic energy in yourself.

There are four seasons in a year with 73 days in each season. There are also four inter-seasons of 18 days each, which correspond to the equinoxes and solstices. Generally, the date which is connected with the coming of the cosmic energy falls in the middle of these 18 days. The acupuncture command point can be used at any time during the 18 days, even though the central date is always the most powerful.

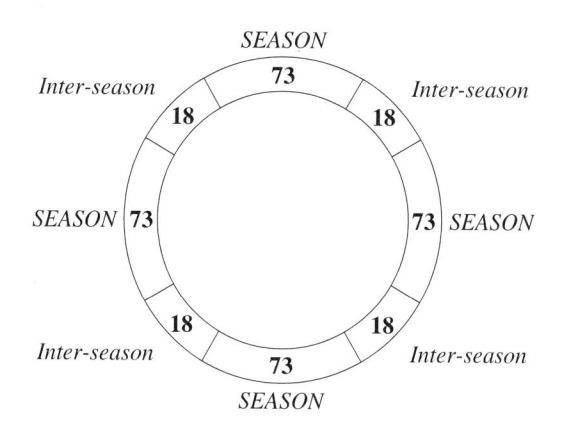

Sound and Acupuncture

ETHERIC CHART (Cosmic Energy) WITH THE MASTER POINTS OF THE EIGHT EXTRA MERIDIANS

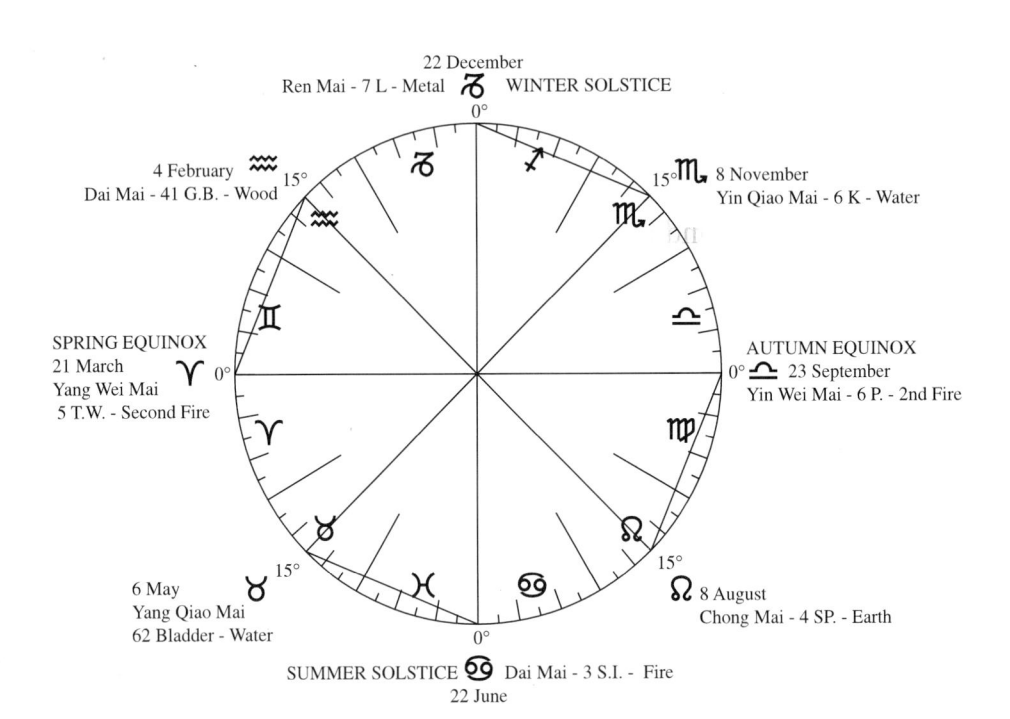

Date		Meridian	Acupoint		Element		Astrology
22	December	Ren Mai	7	L	Metal	0	Capricorn
4	February	Dai Mai	41	G.B.	Wood	15	Aquarius
21	March	Yang Wei Mai	5	T.W.	Fire	0	Aries
6	May	Yang Qiao Mai	62	BL	Water	15	Taurus
22	June	Dai Mai	3	S.I.	Fire	0	Cancer
8	August	Chong Mai	4	SP	Earth	15	Leo
23	September	Yin Wei Mai	6	P	Fire	0	Libra
8	November	Yin Qiao Mai	6	K	Water	15	Scorpio

The dates on the Zodiac Axis that face each other are called the Axes of Cosmic Ancestral Energy. They are reported on earth in geographic terms. For example, the Pisces - Virgo Axis is in the East, starting in the Himalayas and continuing in a straight line to the Island of Bermuda. On this axis, according to Alice Bailey, the Invisible Masters meet in order to bring in new information for the good of humanity.

THE ETHERIC CHART

When we have seen the theoretical and energetic underpinnings of incarnation, as explained in the three steps of synchronization, integration and transformation we can begin to understand this etheric chart. The divination chart itself involves a process of determining the five aspects which shape and move all facets of our lives. These aspects are:

1. HOUR OF BIRTH - Linked with Earth Energy. This hour will give the element of the meridian which commands the energy of the organ at birth. For example, a baby born at 5:00 a.m. is born at the hour where the energy of the body is moving from the lungs into the large intestine. This energy will be affected, then, by the type of birth (whether it was easy or difficult) resulting in either strong or weak lungs/large intestine energy. So the time of birth will reveal which energy is most affected by determining which energy is running at that time. The element linked with a 5:00 a.m. birth would be water in the East and air or metal in the West.

2. SEASON - Linked with Earth Energy. The season of birth determines the element. For example, late summer relates to earth, spring corresponds to the wood element and so on.

3. ASTROLOGICAL SIGN - Linked with Sky Energy. The date of birth will provide the astrological element which is different depending on whether you were born in the East or the West.

4. COSMIC ENERGY - Linked with Sky Energy. The date of birth corresponds to one of the eight dates on the Cosmic Energy Chart (on page 118), and to the special acupuncture point given for each date.

5. QUALITY OF THE YEAR - The year of birth will give the quality of the energy of this aspect. The chart on page 125 in the Appendix gives the general energy quality of each year from 1900 to 2000.

READING THE CHART

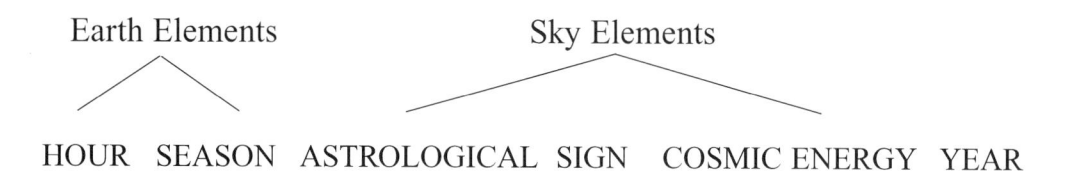

```
Earth Elements           Sky Elements
   /\                    /―――――\
HOUR  SEASON  ASTROLOGICAL SIGN  COSMIC ENERGY  YEAR
```

Analyze the elements obtained at the two levels, physical and spiritual (earth and sky). An understanding of the different aspects given by the six qualities of the sky and the five elements of the earth gives a picture of the roots of each person's temperament, typology and role in life.

For example a child born at 5:00 a.m. on May 3, 1972, will have these two earth elements in his chart:

<u>Metal</u> for the hour   Lungs, Large Intestine   = *Metal*
<u>Wood</u> for the season   Spring   = *Wood*

The sky elements, composed of his astrological sign and cosmic energy would be *Earth* and *Water* - <u>*Earth*</u>, because he was born under the Earth sign Taurus and *Water* for his cosmic energy because the closest date on the Etheric Chart to his birthday would be May 6 (Yang Qiao Mai - 62 Bladder - Water).

The year energy would be <u>*Fire*</u> because the equality of energy in the year 1972 was Shao Yin or fire as seen on page 125.

His chart would be established as follows:

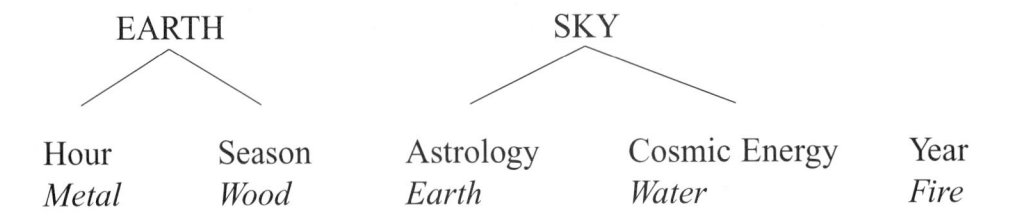

```
        EARTH                        SKY
       /     \                    /        \
Hour      Season        Astrology    Cosmic Energy     Year
Metal     Wood          Earth        Water             Fire
```

From this chart we would analyze the interactions between the earth and the sky elements, taking into account all of the qualities of the five elements as explained in Chapter One, and make the synthesis with the year quality element. The reading could be made on different levels to include physical, psychological and spiritual assets, challenges and tendencies. An example of this reading would be as follows:

EARTH ELEMENTS

Hour: The person was born at 5:00 a.m. during the time when the large intestine, corresponding to the metal element, was beginning to receive energy. Depending upon the degree of difficulty of the birth, the large intestine energy will be strong or weak. An easy birth will give a strong organ, a traumatic birth will weaken the energy of the organ of the hour.

Season: The season of birth was spring, corresponding to the wood element. Spring is the season of joyous awakening from the cold of winter. Spring flowers send their gifts of fragrance into the air and the earth begins to green again. The wood element will be strong in this person and he will express the rich creativity which the wood element supports.

So far we have two elements in the chart, metal of the hour of birth and wood corresponding to the season of birth. The relationship between the metal and the wood elements in this person could prove challenging: in nature, metal cuts wood. He will have to be careful that his large intestine energy, the metal aspect is balanced and not in excess. Excess energy of the metal element will cut the energy of his wood-supported creativity.

SKY ELEMENTS

Astrology: The month of May corresponds to the sign of the Taurus, an earth sign. (We should also take into account the ascendant if possible).

Cosmic Energy: Each person's birthday corresponds to one of the eight directions and eight dates where cosmic energy is manifested strongly on earth. Here this person's birthday falls closest to May 6, which, as you see on the Cosmic Energy Chart of page 118, is the water element. The water element in cosmic energy brings a soft quality, diplomacy, the ability to flow around problems, the ability to listen just as a psychologist might do.

The earth in the astrology will produce the tendency to absorb the sensitive water of the cosmic energy. If this person had water occurring first in the astrology and earth as the cosmic energy, the water would nourish the earth and his life might have been smoother - but the challenges in life are always sources of growth! In this case, we have two challenges, the metal cuts the wood and the earth absorbs the water.

The play between the Earth elements and the Sky elements of the chart will determine which challenges will be mirrored during the course of the lifetime.

Year Energy: The year 1972 is a Shao Yin year where the element Fire predominates. (We find this year quality in the chart on page 125). This fire will link and give a certain coloration to the four other elements. Fire helps water become steam - it makes water more fine. And steam and earth will merge easier than water and earth. Fire also helps to burn the wood, to transmute the wood creativity into more subtle creativity which offer less matter which the metal can cut.

The way the five elements combine in this chart of divination will make it easy to understand character or life patterns which at first seem complex or difficult to appreciate. It is also possible, when you know which elements are missing in your own chart, to look for them in other people or in different situations of life.

With this new esoteric and practical tool for divination, we incorporate acupuncture, the Law of the Five Elements and astrology in order to place the human being in resonance with nature and the cosmos.

Sound and Acupuncture

ENERGY QUALITY OF EACH YEAR

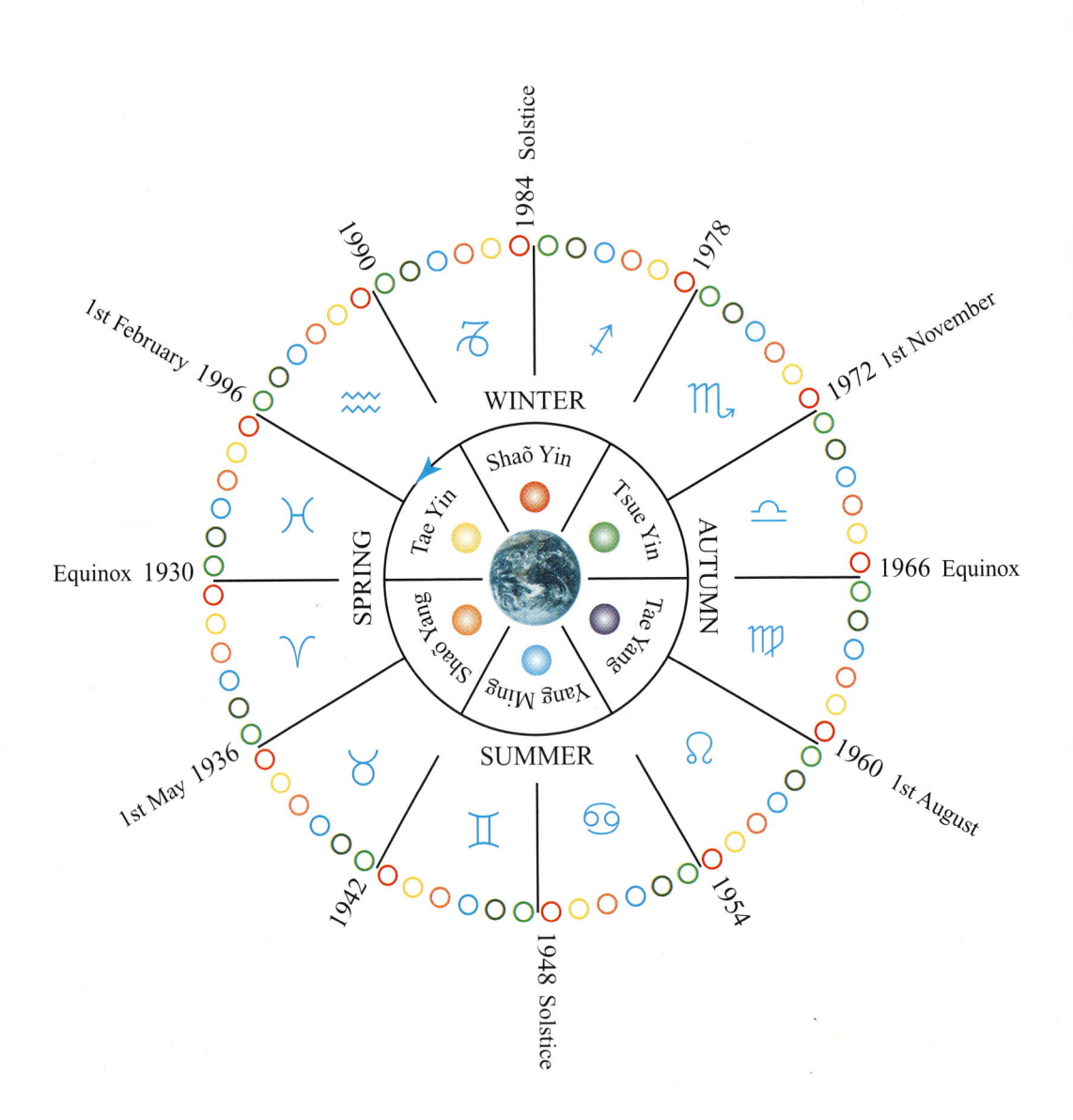

124

Year Quality Energy from 1900 to 2000

TSUE YIN	Wood/fire	1995 1989 1983 1977 1971 1965 1959 1953 1947 1941 1935 1929 1923 1917 1911 1905
SHAO YIN	Fire/water	1996 1990 1984 1978 1972 1966 1960 1954 1948 1942 1936 1930 1924 1918 1912 1906 1900
TAE YIN	Earth/metal	1997 1991 1985 1979 1973 1967 1961 1955 1949 1943 1937 1931 1925 1919 1913 1907 1901
SHAO YANG	Fire/wood	1998 1992 1986 1980 1974 1968 1962 1956 1950 1944 1938 1932 1926 1920 1914 1908 1902
YANG MING	Metal/earth	1999 1993 1987 1981 1975 1969 1963 1957 1951 1945 1939 1933 1927 1921 1915 1909 1903
TAE YANG	Water/fire	2000 1994 1988 1982 1976 1970 1964 1958 1952 1946 1940 1934 1928 1922 1916 1910 1904

APPENDIX

The Mystical Axis
The Ancient Brain as the "New Age" Liver

I include a special mention about liver problems because they are very common today. The source of liver imbalance is difficult to detect because this organ functions on many different levels.

The liver is linked with the element wood. Wood is linked with the "Tree of Life" of the human being. The liver, cut longitudinally reveals the shape of a tree. The essence, wood, makes the liver a link between the spiritual and the physical, just as a tree has its roots in the earth and its branches in the sky.

Many people present a liver imbalance through a gall bladder problem. They try many remedies, diets, etc., and still the problem remains unchanged. There are two reasons for this. The first is that the liver is the center of the Mystical Axis, which is an energy arriving through the Crown, going through the liver and then going out through the sexual organs in a right angle back to the universe. When everything is flowing well, the energy does not stop in any one of the three places. When there is an imbalance, energy can be stuck in the head, in the liver or in the sexual organs, creating imbalance. This Mystical Axis works with spiritual awareness. If we do not capture the spiritual information, it will be difficult to heal these three levels of the wood imbalance and specifically the liver.

The second reason for the difficulty in healing a liver imbalance is that, according to Rudolf Steiner, the liver was the ancient brain before our actual brain was developed. As the master of the organs of the body, it was a strong center for sensing vibration. This is related to the epoch when human beings, in early Lemurian times, had a sensitive body, or a "body of sensitivity" which predated the actual astral body. The liver functioned then almost like a brain.

Today the mental is extremely developed. When people, perhaps arriving at middle age, begin to give up on their social aims and purpose and drive to complete projects in the present, they delegate unconsciously these thoughts to the liver. The liver is then left carrying all of this unfinished business of the brain. This leaves it overcharged with too much energy.

Many people today who are on a spiritual path may have these problems because the spiritual quest sometimes takes one out of a strong focus in the present. They look to the past or future. As long as they have difficulty being in the present, they will find it impossible to be grounded like their "Tree of Life" and can develop a yang deficiency in the wood element of the body.

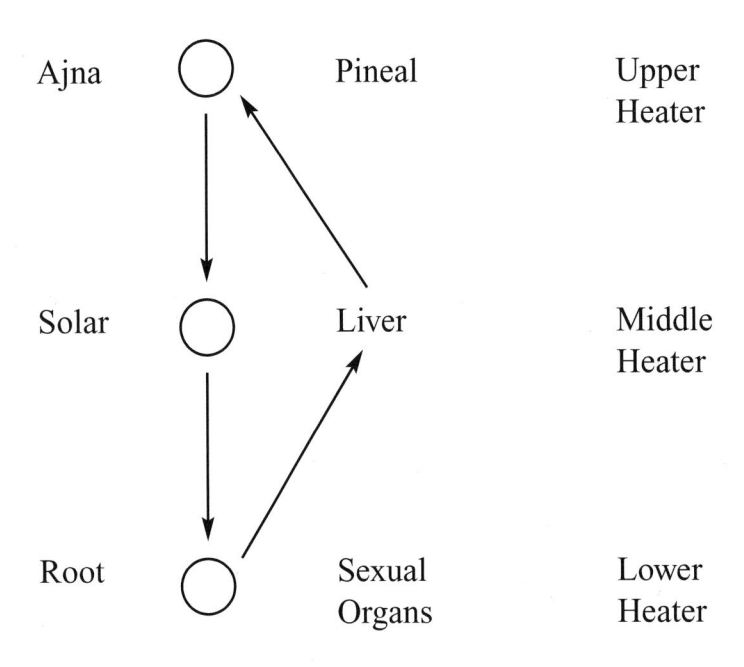

Ajna	Pineal	Upper Heater
Solar	Liver	Middle Heater
Root	Sexual Organs	Lower Heater

The Three Heaters of the Body
Mystical Axis

BRAIN

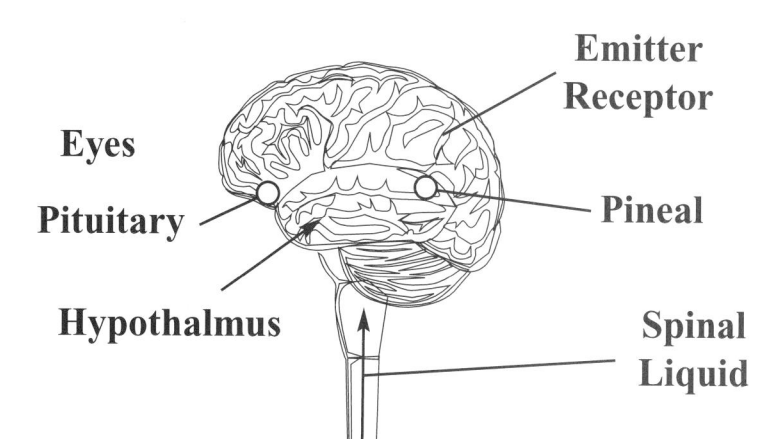

- Emitter Receptor
- Eyes
- Pituitary
- Pineal
- Hypothalmus
- Spinal Liquid

A Note About Pineal Gland

The Pineal Gland could be called the regulator of all glands. Meditators know that the stimulation and awakening of the Pineal Gland initiates new states of consciousness.

The Pineal Gland produces the hormone melatonin which is currently being researched for its "anti-aging, anti-cancer, anti-stress," qualities.

"The Pineal Gland is like an atomic battery; its awakening provokes the birth of our inner sun. When we close our eyes the Pineal Gland becomes active, recharging the intragalactic universe"

Boris de Bardo

RAISING THE ENERGY

Footnotes

1 Veith, Ilza: *The Yellow Emperor's Classic of Internal Medicine*, Berkeley: The University of California Press, 1949. Translation of the *Nei Ching Su Wên*.

2 Veith, Ilza: *The Yellow Emperor's Classic of Internal Medicine*

3 Book II of this series, *Raising Human Frequencies,: The Way of Chi and the Subtle Bodies* discusses chi in detail.

4 Veith, Ilza: *The Yellow Emperor's Classic of Internal Medicine*

5 Ibid

6 The different kinds of chi are described in Book II.

7 See Book II of this series for descriptions of Ancestral, Innate and Acquired Chi.

8 See Chapter Three.

9 Overtones are discussed in Book I of this series, *The Role of Music in the Twenty-First Century.*

10 See Book I, *The Role of Music in the Twenty-First Century.*

11 Actually, it could be said that there are eight temperaments because the Yang Ming temperament and the Tae Yang temperament each can be divided into two tendencies.

12 For more information on the qualities of the musical intervals, see Book I of this series: *The Role of Music in the Twenty-First Century.*

13 Sternheimer, Joel, *"Les Musique des Particules Elementaire."* (brevette deposited with CNRS - National Center for Scientific Research) - Paris, 1988

14 These Musical Modes are discussed in detail in Book I of this series.

15 Kototama sounds are for stimulating organ and meridian energy only. To sedate and purify this energy, use Chinese Breath which is described in Book IV of this series, *Healing with Sound, Color and Movement.*

16 Greek Modes and musical intervals are discussed in detail in Book I of this series, *The Role of Music in the Twenty-First Century.*

About the Author

Fabien Maman is a French musician, composer, acupuncturist, bioenergetician and martial artist. As a musician/composer, he performed many of his original compositions with his quintet in the great concert halls of the world, including Carnegie Hall, the Berlin Philharmonic, the Tokyo Opera and the Paris Olympia.

After an introduction to acupuncture during a musical tour in Japan, he put his performance career on hold in order to study acupuncture with Boris de Bardo in Paris. He was also a student of Sensei Nakazono who first brought Kototama, Science of Pure Sound, to the West.

Fabien Maman became an acupuncturist in 1977 and then linked music and acupuncture by discovering the musical frequencies of the acupuncture shu points. He developed a system which uses tuning forks instead of acupuncture needles.

In 1981, Fabien began a one and a half year experiment with biologist Hélène Grimal of the University of Jussieu in Paris to study the effect of sound in human cells. During the following years, he created several systems of healing which draw on his research with energy, sound, color and movement.

In 1987, Fabien Maman founded The Academy of Sound, Color and Movement, which offers the essence of his research in a practical form. In addition to their studies, each season the Academy students perform a harmonizing concert tuned with the musical key, mode and energy of the season in order to bring performers and audience into resonance with the vibration of earth and cosmic energies.

Fabien lives in the South of France and teaches courses from the Academy throughout the world.

Tama-Dō Press

For further information about the work of Fabien Maman, including CDs, audio and video cassettes, and workshops, please contact:

The Academy of Sound, Color and Movement
2060 Las Flores Canyon
Malibu, CA 90265
800.615.3675
info@tama-do.com
www.tamado.com